# What you may
# NOT
# know
# ABOUT
# BERMUDA

**by**
**Horst Augustinovic**

**ISBN: 978-1-927750-09-4**

Published by Print Link
P.O. Box HM 937, Hamilton HM DX, Bermuda
Telephone: 441 295-4343  Fax: 441 295-3445  Email: netlink@link.bm

Printed in Canada

# Contents

Do You Know …

# … That the 1609 Wreck of the 'Sea Venture' changed World History?

Following two failed English attempts to establish settlements in North America – the Roanoke Colony in Virginia and the Popham Colony in Maine – the Jamestown settlement was established in Virginia in 1607. The following year two supply missions were sent from England, however, due to a lack of experience and resources, the colony was threatened by disease, starvation and warfare with Native Americans.

Captain John Smith implored the Virginia Company in London to "…send but thirty carpenters, husbandmen, gardiners, fishermen, blacksmiths, masons and diggers up of trees, roots, well provided; than a thousand of such awe have: for except wee be able to lodge them and feed them, the most will consume with want of necessaries before they can be made good for anything."

London obviously took note of Captain Smith's plea and decided that the third supply mission would be larger and better equipped than the two previous missions. They even decided to construct a new purpose-built emigrant ship – the 'Sea Venture' – at a cost of £1,500. Displacing 300 tons, the 'Sea Venture' differed substantially from contemporary ships – her guns were placed on the main deck rather than below, which was then the norm.

This meant that the 'Sea Venture' did not have double-timbering and her hold could be sheathed and equipped for passengers. When the ship was launched in 1609 and sent on her maiden voyage to Jamestown on June 2, she may have had a critical flaw: her timbers had not yet set. This proved disastrous when on July 24, the fleet of nine ships ran into a strong storm – probably a hurricane – and the ships were separated.

After fighting the storm for three days, the caulking of the 'Sea Venture' was forced from between her timbers and the ship began to leak rapidly. Although everyone aboard was bailing, the water in the hold had risen to nine feet and both passengers and crew gave up all hope of survival. It was at that point when Admiral Sir George Somers, at the helm of the ship, saw land and deliberately sailed the 'Sea Venture' onto the reefs to prevent her from foundering and allowing all 150 people aboard to get on land safely.

The survivors were fortunate to salvage parts and timbers from the 'Sea Venture' and soon built two new ships, the 'Deliverance' and 'Patience'. While building the two ships, the longboat of the 'Sea Venture' was fitted with a mast and sent to find Virginia. Unfortunately the boat and crew were never seen again. On May 10, 1610, the 'Deliverance' and 'Patience' finally set sail with all survivors and laden with supplies such as salted pork, leaving behind only two mutineers.

*The Bermuda Post Office has issued two sets of stamps regarding the 'Sea Venture'. Shown here is the fleet of nine ships leaving Plymouth, England, and the flagship 'Sea Venture' wrecked on Bermuda's reefs.*

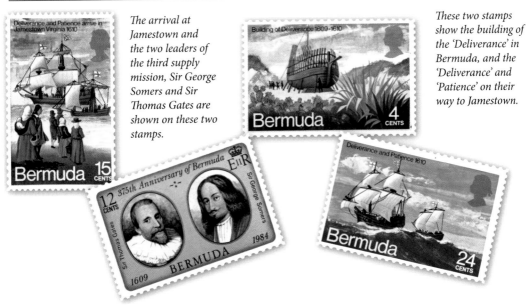

The arrival at Jamestown and the two leaders of the third supply mission, Sir George Somers and Sir Thomas Gates are shown on these two stamps.

These two stamps show the building of the 'Deliverance' in Bermuda, and the 'Deliverance' and 'Patience' on their way to Jamestown.

On arrival in Jamestown on May 23, the survivors' ordeal did not end, however, as only 60 of the 500 settlers were found alive and the settlement of Jamestown was considered unviable and hopeless. On June 10 everybody was boarded onto the 'Deliverance' and 'Patience' and the two ships began to make their way back to England. As they sailed down the James River, they were met by the arrival of yet another relief fleet – three ships under the command of the new military governor, Baron De La Warre.

With new hope, Jamestown was granted a reprieve and the settlers were re-landed. Under strong leadership, the settlers' fate soon changed for the better. They found food, improved their security and soon began to plant tobacco, producing the first profitable crop by 1614 and securing the success of the colony.

Had the 'Sea Venture' sank in that 1609 hurricane, would Jamestown have survived without the leadership of Admiral Sir George Somers, Lieutenant-General Sir Thomas Gates, Captain Christopher Newport, Sylvester Jordain and William Strachey? Probably not.

So the wreck of the 'Sea Venture' not only began Bermuda's 400 years of permanent settlement, but altered the fate of Jamestown, England's first successful foothold in the Americas, changing the New World forever.

'Ventura ad Marem', the figure head of the 'Sea Venture', was the symbol of venture at sea. A mythical animal with the head of a hound and the scales of a fish, this ancient Sea Dog was used as a talisman by Phoenicians as early as 700 B.C.

Officially the Coat of Arms of Bermuda features a red lion holding a shield showing an earlier shipwreck. I'd like to think that it is a Sea Dog and the 'Sea Venture' that are featured on Bermuda's Coat of Arms. 'Quo Fata Ferunt' appropriately translates as 'Whither the Fates Carry Us'.

Do You Know …

# … How Bermuda's Nine Parishes were established and who they are named after?

Following the accidental settlement of Bermuda on July 28th 1609 by the survivors of the 'Sea Venture', the island was at one point occupied by only two, and later three, men. It wasn't until 1612 with the arrival of 'The Plough' from England, that Bermuda was deliberately colonized and a Governor – Richard Moore – established. In 1616 Captain Daniel Tucker, after spending five years in Virginia, became Governor of Bermuda.

An initial survey of Bermuda had began by Governor Moore, however, it was Governor Tucker who in 1616 called upon Richard Norwood to make a detailed survey and divide the island into eight Tribes, each sub-divided into fifty 25-acre plots. (The Bermuda Charter had specified that one quarter of the land was to be public land and this included St. George's Island, St. David's Island, Longbird Island, Smith's Island, Cooper's Island, Coney Island, Nonsuch Island, as well as a small portion at the eastern end of the Main Island).

Richard Norwood had quite a task, calculating the exact size of the proposed eight Tribes from the remaining land, especially when considering that the island was covered in dense cedar forests, that there

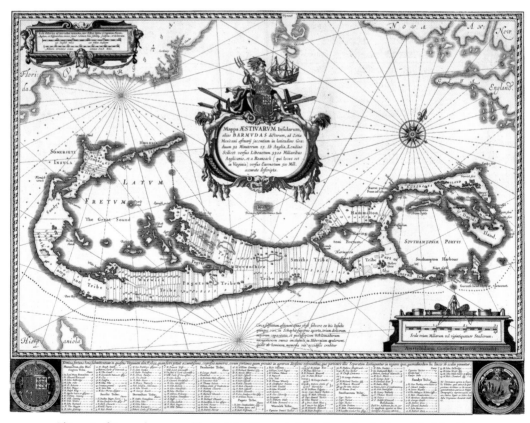

*This map of Bermuda engraved by Guijelm Blaeuw in 1630 shows the division of the island into eight Tribes and the subdivisions into 25-acre plots. If one person owned more that one plot, the total is shown as one plot and numbered accordingly.*

*The family crests of each 'Gentleman Adventurer' shown here were painted by William Harrington on the occasion of Bermuda's 350th Anniversary for display at the Bermuda Airport.*

were no roads and that 120 islands were included! Still, he came up with eight Tribes of exactly the same size – 2.0355 square miles – each of which was divided into fifty 25-acre plots.

Before sailing back to England with the data for his map in 1617, Richard Norwood became involved in what was known as the 'overplus scandal'. Governor Tucker had been promised three shares of land by the Somers Island Company and Richard Norwood had made allowance for this 'overplus' in his calculations, however, as the survey was done from east to west, Governor Tucker's 'overplus' would fall at the extreme west end of the island.

As Richard Norwood approached the western end of the main island (now Southampton), he informed the Governor that he had seen a beautiful valley of 'fatte and lustye soyle'. Delighted by this news, Governor Tucker abruptly ordered Norwood to continue the survey from the very western end of the island (now Sandys). The official reason for this change in plans was the fact that the western islands had not yet been invaded by rats and it would therefore be easier for Norwood to conduct his survey. Conveniently Governor Tucker's 'overplus' now fell exactly into the area he wanted for himself.

When he proceeded to build a large cedar house at public expense on his 200 acres of land, even the Somers Island Company in London was outraged and threatened to deprive him of his 'overplus' and the house he built at their expense. Fortunately he was able to send a huge consignment of tobacco to London which appeased the company and he was able to retain his now famous house, as well as almost half the property.

The eight Tribes were eventually called Parishes and the eastern islands where Bermuda's development started, became the ninth Parish – St. George's. So who are they named after? In most cases they were Elizabethan aristocrats who considered themselves 'Gentlemen Adventurers' and who were the largest shareholders of their Tribe.

From East to West, St. George's is named after the Patron Saint of England, however, as Sir George Somers was the founder of Bermuda, many consider that St. George's is named after him. Hamilton Parish is named after James Hamilton, 2nd Marquess of Hamilton; Smith's Parish after Sir Thomas Smith; Devonshire after William Cavendish, 1st Earl of Devonshire; Pembroke after William Herbert, 3rd Earl of Pembroke; Paget after William Paget, 4th Lord Paget; Warwick after Robert Rich, 2nd Earl of Warwick; Southampton after Henry Wriothesley, 3rd Earl of Southampton and Sandys after Sir Edwin Sandys.

Do You Know …

# … That Bermuda passed the New World's First Conservation Legislation?

The first book about Bermuda was written in 1610 by Sylvester Jordain, one of the survivors of the 'Sea Venture'. It includes the following descriptions about the abundant wildlife they found on their arrival on the island:

*"Wherefore my opinion sincerely of this Iland is, that whereas it hath beene, and is still accounted, the most dangerous, infortunate, and most forlorne place of the world, it is in truth the richest, healthfullest, and pleasing land..."*

*"Sir George Sommers … found out sufficient of many kind of fishes, and so plentyfull thereof, that in halfe an houre he took so many great fishes with hookes, as did suffice the whole company one day. These fishes are very fat and sweete, and of that proportion and bignesse, that three of them will conueniently lade two men: those we called rock-fish. Besides there are such abundance of Mullets, that with a seane might be taken at one draught one thousand at the least..."*

'*The Countrie affordeth great abundance of Hogges, as that there hath beene taken by Sir George Sommers, who was the first that hunted for them, to the number of two and thirty at one time..."*

*"There is Fowle in great number vpon the Ilands, where they breed, that there hath beene taken in two or three houres, a thousand at the least; the bird being of the bignes of a good Pidgeon, and layeth egges as big as Hen egges vpon the sand, where they come and lay them dayly, although men sit downe amongst them..."*

*"Another Sea fowle there is that lyeth in little holes in the ground, like vnto a cony-hole, and are in great numbers, exceeding good meate, very fat and sweet (those we had in the winter) and their eggs are white, and of that bignesse, that they are not to be knowne from Hen egges."*

*"There are also great store of Tortoses, (which some call Turtles) and those so great, that I haue seene a bushel of egges in one of their bellies, which are sweeter then any Henne egge: and the Tortose it selfe is all very good meate, and yeeldeth great store of oyle, which is as sweete as any butter; and one of them will suffice fifty men a meale, at the least: and of these hath beene taken great store, with two boates, at the least forty in one day."*

'*There are also great Plentie of Whales, which I conceaue are verie easie to be killed, for they come so vsually, and ordinarily to the shore, that we heard them oftentimes in the night a bed; and haue seene many of them neare the shoare, in the day time."*

Within only a few short years the early settlers had so depleted certain species, that in 1619 an Act was passed against the killing of young turtles. This is considered to be the New World's earliest written conservation legislation. Unfortunately the settlers did not know that sea turtles take up to 50 years to mature.

## An act against the killinge of ouer young Tortoyses.

In regard that much waste and abuse hath been offered and yet is by sundrye lewd and impvident psons inhabitinge wthin these Islands who in there continuall goinges out to sea for fish doe upon all occasions, And at all tymes as they can meete with them, snatch & catch up indifferentlye all kinds of Tortoyses both yonge & old little and greate and soe kill carrye awaye and devoure them to the much decay of the breed of so excellent a fishe the daylye skarringe of them from of our shores and the danger of an utter distroyinge and losse of them.

It is therefore enacted by the Authoritie of this present Assembly That from hence forward noe manner of pson or psons of what degree or condition soeuer he be inhabitinge or remaining at any time wthin these Islands shall pesume to kill or cause to be killed in any Bay Sound Harbor or any other place out to Sea: being wthin five leagues round about of those Islands any young Tortoyses that are or shall not be found to be Eighteen inches in the Breadth or Dyameter and that upon the penaltye for euerye such offence of the fforfeyture of fifteen pounds of Tobacco whereof the one half is to be bestowed in publique uses the other upon the Informer.

Almost 400 years after the passing of this Act against the killing of young turtles, Bermuda has established 'The Bermuda Turtle Project', a research and education programme sponsored by the Bermuda Aquarium, Museum and Zoo and the Sea Turtle Conservancy located in Florida.

Surrounded by lush seagrass beds and unpolluted waters, Bermuda provides the perfect habitat for young green turtles and hawksbills. It is the ideal site where immature green turtles can be studied in their natural habitat.

Do You Know …

# … That the first proposal for a College in Bermuda was made in 1722?

George Berkeley, Bishop of Cloyne, Ireland, in a letter dated March 4th 1722 to Lord Percival, announced his intention to establish a "theology and fine arts college" in Bermuda and "it is now about ten months since I have determined with myself to spend the residue of my days in the Island of Bermuda, where I trust in Providence I may be the mean instrument of doing good to mankind".

*Bishop George Berkeley*

Three years later, in 1725, he published a paper entitled "A Proposal for the better Supplying of Churches in our Foreign Plantations, and for converting the Savage Americans to Christianity, by a College to be erected in the Summer Islands, otherwise called The Isles of Bermuda".

Bishop Berkeley had received much information about Bermuda from clergymen who had served here, and although he never travelled to Bermuda himself, he offered in his Proposal an amazingly detailed description of Bermuda, the landscape, beauties, resources, prosperity, and inhabitants. Here are a few excerpts:

'The climate is by far the healthiest and most serene, and consequently the most fit for study'. 'There is the greatest abundance of all the necessary provisions for life, which is much to be considered in a place for education'. 'It is the securest spot in the universe, being environed round with rocks, with all but two narrow entrances, both well guarded by forts, which render it inaccessible to pirates or enemies. It would therefore be impossible to find anywhere a more secure retreat for students'.

At the time Bishop Berkeley was convinced that Europe was in spiritual decline and that the New World offered hope for a new golden age. Having secured a charter and promises of funding from the British Parliament, he sailed to America in 1728 and spent three years in Newport, Rhode Island, waiting for the promised funds. Unfortunately his political support in England collapsed and he was forced to abandon his idea of a Bermuda College and returned to Ireland.

In 1853 a collegiate institute known as St. Paul's School had opened in Hamilton in an ultimately unsuccessful attempt to revive the scheme that Bishop Berkeley had conceived well over a century before. A 'Berkeley Club' remained from this project, and in 1879, seven coloured Bermudians founded an educational society which, to memorialize Bishop George Berkeley, they decided to call "The Berkeley Educational Society". From this developed the Berkeley Institute of today.

Meanwhile in 1868, California passed an act to "Create and Organize the University of California." This "seat of learning" was born through a merger of two fledgling institutions — the private College of California, in Oakland, and the Agricultural, Mining, and Mechanical Arts College, located four miles north, at a town named after Bishop George Berkeley.

It is ironic that, although unsuccessful with his "Bermuda Scheme", Bishop Berkeley should now have both one of Bermuda's Senior Schools, as well as one of America's best-known Universities named after him.

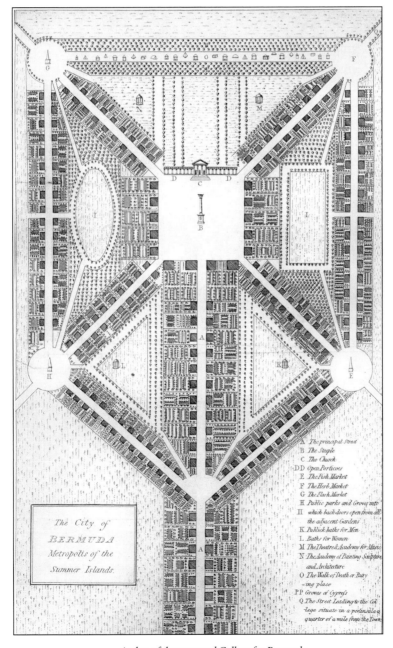

*A plan of the proposed College for Bermuda*

Do You Know …

# … What George Washington promised the people of Bermuda in 1775?

The thirteen American colonies that rebelled against Britain, were just as English as Bermudians, who regularly traded with those colonies, had family living in the American colonies and sent their children to school in America. It should not be surprising that public opinion in Bermuda was very much divided in regard to the American quest for independence from England.

The British, who knew that Bermudians traded with America, tried to put a stop to that trade, with Bermudians coming close to starvation as a consequence. As the situation became more critical, the Bermuda Government sent Colonel Henry Tucker to Philadelphia to try and negotiate a deal with the Continental Congress, trading salt in exchange for food.

*General George Washington, later to become the first President of the United States of America.*

Unfortunately the Continental Congress was not interested in such a deal. What they were interested in, however, was the gunpowder which the British were storing in Bermuda. They made it clear to Colonel Tucker, that any ship arriving in America with British gunpowder, would return to Bermuda stacked with provisions!

On August 14th, 1775, two weeks after Colonel Tucker's return to Bermuda, two ships appeared off Tobacco Bay in St. George's. Manning small boats, crew members approached the gunpowder magazine which had been built a couple of years earlier. After cutting a hole in the roof to gain access, they rolled a hundred barrels of gunpower down the hill to the waiting boats. 1,800 pounds of powder was landed in Philadelphia a week later, the rest sent to Charleston, South Carolina.

By the time the theft was discovered, it was too late to pursue the powder-laden ships. Capt. John Dill, a known sympathizer of the Americans and whose property overlooked the area, maintained his innocence when questioned by the Governor's men. "But you could hardly miss seeing the ships off the North Shore!" "No," said Dill, "I was reading my Bible!"

Not realizing that the gunpowder had already been stolen, George Washington wrote the following letter:

*To the Inhabitants of the Islands of Bermuda*

*Gentlemen,*

*In the great conflict which agitates the continent, I cannot doubt but the asserters of freedom and the right of the constitution are possessed of your most favorable regards and wishes for success.*

*As descendants of freedom, and heirs with us of the same glorious inheritance – we flatter ourselves, that, though divided by situation, we are firmly united in sentiment. The cause of virtue and liberty is confined to no continent or climate – it comprehends, within its capacious limits, the wise and good, however dispersed and separated in space and distance.*

*You will not be uninformed, that the violence and rapacity of a tyrannic ministry have forced the citizens of America, your brother colonists, into arms. We equally detest and lament the prevalence of those counsels,* which have led to the effusion of so much human blood and left us with no alternative but a civil war – or a base submission. The wise Disposer of all events has hitherto smiled upon our virtuous efforts. These mercenary troops, a few of whom lately boasted of subjugating this vast continent, have been checked in their earliest ravages, and are now actually encircled in a small space, their Arms disgraced, and suffering all the calamities of a siege. The virtue, spirit, and unison of the provinces leave them nothing to fear, but the want of ammunition.

The application of our enemies to foreign states, and their vigilance open our coasts, are the only efforts they have made against us with success. Under the circumstances, and with these sentiments, we have turned our eyes to you, gentlemen, for relief.

We are informed there is a very large magazine on your island under a very feeble guard – We would not wish to involve an opposition, in which, from your situation, we would be unable to support you; we know not, therefore, to what extent to solicit your assistance in availing ourselves of this supply; but, if your favour and friendship to North America and its liberties have not been misrepresented, I persuade myself – you may, consistently with your own safety, promote and further the scheme, so as to give it the fairest prospect of success.

*Be assured that in this case the whole power and exertion of my influence will be made with the honourable Continental Congress, that your island may not only be supplied with provisions, but experience every mark of affection and friendship, which the grateful citizens of a free country can bestow on its bretheren and benefactors.*

*General George Washington, Camp Cambridge,*
*three miles from Boston, Sept. 6, 1775*

Having received the gunpowder from Bermuda, the Continental Congress lifted the embargo against supplying provisions to Bermuda and an agreement was reached to again ship salt to America.

*On October 27th, 1975, Bermuda issued four stamps to commemorate the Gunpowder Plot of 1775. This resulted in several fiery Letters to the Editor of the Royal Gazette, complaining that such a treasonable act should not have been commemorated on postage stamps. The final act was the dismissal of the Chairman of the Stamp Design Advisory Committee, Mr. Donald E. Gibbons.*

Do You Know …

# … About Bermuda's role in the use of Biological Warfare during the American Civil War?

Several attempts to use biological warfare by the Confederates against Union forces were reported during the Civil War. One such plot was by Dr. Luke Blackburn, a Southern sympathizer from Kentucky, who in 1864 plotted to sell yellow fever infected clothing in Washington, D.C. and several other cities, in an attempt to cause a yellow fever epidemic in the North.

Blackburn's sympathies were very much pro-Confederate. At the outbreak of the Civil War he volunteered to act as agent for the Confederacy and was assigned to organize blockade runners in Canada. When a yellow fever epidemic swept through Bermuda in the spring and summer of 1864, Dr. Blackburn volunteered his services to the Bermuda health authorities. By late October, the disease had abated and the doctor was commended by the Queen's Admiralty for his work. But in April of 1865, Charles Allen, US Consul in Bermuda, uncovered the true purpose of Blackburn's visit to Bermuda – to collect infected clothing and bedding from yellow fever victims and ship the contaminated articles in eight large trunks to the US.

*Dr. Luke Blackburn – humanitarian or yellow-fever conspirator?*

The trunks were actually shipped to another Confederate agent, Godfrey Hyman in Halifax, who was to send them to Washington, D.C. and several other cities and arrange to have their contents sold at auction. Once distributed, Blackburn hoped the contaminated items would create a yellow fever pandemic. There was also a special place for President Lincoln in this plan. Blackburn packed several dress shirts with the infected articles, hoping to cross-contaminate them with yellow fever, and Godfrey Hyman was instructed to deliver them to the White House as a gift to President Lincoln from an anonymous benefactor.

Hyman followed his instructions with the eight trunks, selling them to an auction house in Washington, D.C. and to military contractors in Norfolk and New Bern, but decided not to risk a visit to the White House.

In 1865 Blackburn returned to Bermuda to secure three more trunks of infected clothing, which he intended to sell in New York. This time, however, the scheme was exposed by Blackburn's own stinginess. Rather than pay Hyman the agreed sum of $60,000 for his work, Blackburn stiffed him. Hyman now flipped sides and contacted Union authorities who paid him for the information that exposed several Confederate plots operating out of southern Canada and Bermuda.

# THE GREAT FEVER PLOT

## Examination of the Notorious Dr. Blackburn at Toronto.

---

## THE SWORN STATEMENT OF HYAMS

---

## Complete Revelation of the Conspiracy to Introduce Pestilence.

---

## Dr. Blackburn to be Sent Before the Judges at the Next Assizes.

---

## He Gives Bail to the Amount of $8,000.

*A Toronto newspaper headline of May 24, 1865. The full page article gave complete details of the court proceedings against Dr. Blackburn.*

Union authorities attempted to prosecute Blackburn who wisely refused to return from Canada. Under pressure from the United States, Canadian authorities charged Blackburn in Toronto, but he was acquitted due to a lack of evidence as most of the incriminating evidence was unavailable to Canadian prosecutors.

In 1872, Blackburn returned to Kentucky where he resumed his medical practice and earned widespread applause for his efforts to combat yellow fever outbreaks in Memphis, Florida and Kentucky. Due to his humanitarian efforts he was elected Governor of Kentucky in 1879. Today, Governor Blackburn is remembered as the father of prison reform in the state and his tombstone is inscribed "Luke Pryor Blackburn – the Good Samaritan."

One can only assume that Dr. Blackburn, a physician who always exhibited the highest ethics before and after the Civil War, felt such loyalty for the Confederacy that he lost his regard for human life during that unfortunate period.

Amazingly, Dr. Blackburn's bioterrorism claimed no victims. Understanding infectious diseases was incomplete in the 1860s and it was not realized that yellow fever is spread by mosquitoes and not by contaminated bedding and clothing! So when yellow fever broke out at New Bern shortly after the arrival of the trunk from Bermuda, killing more than 2,000 civilians and soldiers, it was not as a result of Dr. Blackburn's efforts in Bermuda.

Do You Know ...

# ... What's on the bottom of Dolly's Bay in St. David's?

A strange craft appeared one day in 1868 off St. David's. It had neither spars nor sails, just a coating of barnacles. A few St. David's islanders headed out in their sloop Princess Royal to investigate. What they found was a large raft which showed signs of having been in a collision, but nothing to indicate the purpose for which it had been built.

Because of its solid construction of sound timber, the men labouriously towed the raft to Dolly's Bay, hoping to break the huge baulks apart. Because of the many inter-connecting bolts they did not succeed and simply left the raft to the elements in Dolly's Bay.

Four years later, in 1872, Capt. E.H. Faucon, representing Boston underwriters and once master of the brig Pilgrim, came to Bermuda and immediately recognized the derelict raft. As an auxiliary officer of the United States Navy and commander of the steamer Ericsson, Capt. Faucon, in January 1863, towed four torpedo rafts from New York to Charleston, S.C., where they were to be used in naval operations against the Confederates.

Off Cape Hatteras the Ericsson ran into a gale and, during the night, one of the rafts broke away. At dawn the crew looked in vain for the raft, as well as a young seaman who had been swept overboard. Unfortunately neither was found and the torpedo raft began a six-year journey before being discovered off Bermuda.

So what was the purpose of the raft? In order to deter Union naval forces during the Civil War,

*The Civil War Raft in Dolly's Bay in the 1890's ...*

*… and more recently at low tide*

the Confederates deployed underwater mines, also called torpedos at the time. In response the Federals built heavy torpedo-searching rafts to clear paths through the mine fields of Charleston Harbour. The rafts were constructed to fit the bow of a vessel and were secured by chains from ringbolts on the ship to ringbolts on the raft.

The first use of an anti-torpedo raft was in April 1863 at Charleston. The ironclad Weehawken, with a raft attached to her bow, led eight other ships in the attack. As Weehawken approached the obstructions, they proved too formidable and Capt. John Rodgers turned his ship out to sea. The raft was now pitching and colliding with the bow of the Weehawken and when it started to damage the bow, Capt. Rodgers cut the raft adrift.

Capt. Rodgers report of this incident includes the following: "…it was found that the sea converted the raft into a huge battering ram, which shook the vessel at every undulation" and "It is obvious that with the pitching which always accompanies a swell, the two bodies would be brought into collision with a power proportionate to their weight. The raft displaces about 90 tons and its motions did not at all correspond with the motions of the vessel. The raft rose while the vessel fell, and the reverse."

What is left of the 'Civil War Raft' in Dolly's Bay today is just a small part of the original raft and a reminder of one of the least successful designs in naval history.

## Do You Know …

*Bermuda's first newspaper, The Bermuda Gazette of January 17, 1784.*

# … About Bermuda's First Newspaper?

In 1771 Bermuda's House of Assembly resolved unanimously to "give all possible Encouragement to any capable Person who may come to these Islands and establish a proper Press".

Isaiah Thomas, one of America's most prominent printers, had married Mary Dill, daughter of Joseph Dill of Bermuda. In 1772, when American politics were very difficult, especially to a newspaper editor, Isaiah Thomas considered relocating from Boston to Bermuda. He wrote to his father-in-law:

*"Sir, After so long a silence which has been entirely owing to the want of an opportunity, I beg leave to address you on the subject of a Printing office being established in the Island of Bermuda, previous to this I would inform your Honor, that I received your very kind Letter about 18 months ago, which I did myself the Honor of answering by one Capt. Cooper of your Island, but his Vessel and cargo being entirely lost the Letters perished with them. I carry on the printing Business in this metropolis, and have no reason*

*to complain of my success; but there are some circumstances which would make me willing to quit my engagement here, if I could be encouraged in Bermuda…"*

Unfortunately nothing became of this proposal and Isaiah Thomas continued publishing the *Massachusetts Spy* and built up the most important printing and publishing business of his time in America.

In 1781, Henry Tucker "observed to the House that certain individuals sensible to the great advantages that would be derived to the public from the establishment of a press within these Islands, had resolved by subscription within themselves to furnish the Sum necessary thereto…" Two years later, on March 18,1783, it was 'Resolved that in the Supply Bill now before the House Certificates for a sum not exceeding Four hundred and fifty pounds Currency be issued from the Public treasury to certain Trustees to be by them apply'd by loan or otherwise to effect the Establishment of a Press within these Islands as speedily as may be, they becoming accountable to the Legislature therefor'.

After Bermuda's Legislature voted the sum of £450 to set up a printing press in Bermuda, Joseph Stockdale was brought out from England to print the laws made by the Legislature, as well as the proceedings of the House of Assembly. These accounts became Bermuda's first newspaper.

This note of thanks to the Gentlemen of Bermuda was included in the first issue:

*"The printer begs leave to return his hearty and unfeigned Thanks to the Gentlemen of Bermuda, for the very flattering encouragement he has received since his arrival amongst them: His poor endeavours shall be exerted to merit their future esteem; and he flatters himself he shall contribute a little to keep up a spirit of harmony and innocent entertainment, industriously avoiding even a hint, by which any worthy individual may, in the least, be prejudiced".*

Joseph Stockdale died in 1803. His daughters Frances, Pricilla and Sarah continued to print and publish *The Bermuda Gazette* until 1816 when it was continued by Charles Rollin Beach who had married Sarah. Publication seized in 1824.

*In 1984, on the occasion of the 200th anniversary of Joseph Stockdale's arrival in Bermuda, the Bermuda Post Office issued these commemorative stamps – Joseph Stockdale in front of his print shop in St. George's and the printing press on which he printed* The Bermuda Gazette.

Do You Know …

*The only known copy of the Royal Gazette published on January 8th, 1828*

# … About the Beginnings of the Royal Gazette?

The strained relations between Governor John Hodgson and Charles Rollin Beach, publisher of Bermuda's first newspaper *The Bermuda Gazette* at the time, led to Mr. Beach leaving Bermuda in 1924. His departure left Bermuda without a newspaper. In fact Governor Hodgson was so displeased with Mr. Beach that as early as 1809 he brought Edmund Ward to Bermuda to start a rival newspaper to *The Bermuda Gazette*. This was to become the first *Royal Gazette*.

Unfortunately Edmund Ward run afoul of the next Governor, Sir James Cockburn, who removed his commission as 'King's Printer' in 1816 and forced Mr. Ward to return to Halifax where he continued to publish a newspaper. This brought an end to Bermuda's first *Royal Gazette* and it would be another twelve years before the present *Royal Gazette* started publication in 1828.

It was the next Governor, Sir William Lumley, who authorized a one-time payment of £500 to bring Donald McPhee Lee as "Printer to the King's Most Excellent Majesty" to Bermuda.

*Donald McPhee Lee who published the Royal Gazette for 55 years*

Donald McPhee Lee was born in Charlottetown, Prince Edward Island, in 1804. Robert Lee, his father, was Commissary General with the military and stationed in Bermuda. It seems that he successfully put forward his son's name as 'King's Printer' following the turbulent period of Sir William Lumley.

Having embarked at Halifax on October 29th, 1827 in the Bermuda schooner *Sally Ann*, his eleven-week voyage to Bermuda was a harrowing experience to say the least. The Captain of the *Sally Ann* became blind, the mate was illiterate and could not navigate, and the *Sally Ann* was painted in a colour used by pirates, with the result that passing ships refused any help. Captain W.E. Meyer tells the story of this trip in some detail in his book 'Wrecked on the Bermudas'.

With Donald McPhee Lee missing for months and presumed dead, his brother David Ross Lee produced the first two issues of the *Royal Gazette* on January 8th and 15th, 1928. Once Donald McPhee Lee arrived, he produced the third issue on January 22, in a larger four-page format, using the new type he had brought from Halifax. He continued to publish the *Royal Gazette* for the next 55 years, until just two weeks before his death in 1883.

It is interesting that the very first issue of the *Royal Gazette* included the following promise that 'The pages of the *Royal Gazette* will never be profaned by the scandals of private malice or the bitterness of party contention; but will be devoted to extracts from the most approved literature of the day and to the best original compositions that can be obtained within the Colony'.

Do You Know …

## … About the First Bermuda Books?
## Part 1 – Richard Cotter – 'Sketches of Bermuda, *or* Somers' Islands'

Richard Cotter was born in County Cork, Ireland, in 1776 and joined the Royal Navy when 20 years old. In 1806 he married Ellen Young and they had 8 children. Richard Cotter died in 1834 while in the Royal Navy Reserve.

In 1824 he was appointed Purser on *H.M.S President* and was stationed in Bermuda. Apparently he could not find much information about Bermuda before coming to the island and decided that he would write a book about Bermuda while he was stationed here. In his Preface to the 1828 book Richard Cotter wrote:

'*The obscurity in which the Bermuda's, or Somers' Islands, have remained in point of historical facts, since they were first peopled, and my fruitless endeavours to gain information respecting the Colony, on my appointment to a public situation there, four years ago, determined me to glean all I could during a residence of that period.*

*I am free to confess that I had many motives in collecting all I could on a place that at first sight interested me in no trifling degree.*

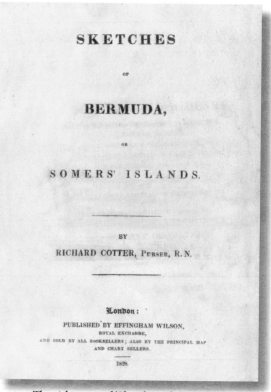

The title page of 'Sketches of Bermuda'.

*The friendly hospitality of the men, the mild and gentle demeanour of the women, that needed not a frown to awe the libertine to respect them, the curiosity natural to a citizen of the world, the wish to become useful to my country, and last, though not least, a desire to make my researches as advantageous as possible to my numerous family, were irresistible inducements, first to collect all the materials I could, and now to trust my feelings and my fate to a generous public.*'

The view from Murray's Anchorage.

A rather simple Map of Bermuda.

A Bermudian Boat.

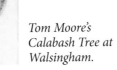

Tom Moore's Calabash Tree at Walsingham.

The 76-page book is very much a view of Bermuda from a naval officer's perspective at the very time when the British Government shipped thousands of convicts from London prisons to Bermuda to build the Royal Navy Dockyard. The book also includes several interesting lithographic illustrations by T.Y. Cotter, presumably a relative.

Bermuda's Dockyard in the 1820s.

Do You Know ...

# ... About the First Bermuda Books?
# Part 2 – Susette Harriet Lloyd – 'Sketches of Bermuda'

Susette Harriet Lloyd visited Bermuda from 1829 to 1831 and stayed with the family of Archdeacon Aubrey George Spencer. During her 2-year stay she wrote a series of letters to her friends in England, many of them concerning local people and their living conditions just prior to emancipation in 1834. On her return to England Susette Harriet Lloyd was urged to publish her letters, resulting in her book 'Sketches of Bermuda'.

In her Preface, she wrote *'The recent changes which have taken place in the legal condition of the negroes in our West India colonies, having rendered any authentic information connected with the subject desirable at the present moment, it is hoped, that the following pages will not be deemed altogether uninteresting, especially since they refer to a country which, though the smallest of all our West India possessions, has attracted a greater degree of attention than others of larger extent, in consequence of its deviation from the emancipation bill, passed by the mother country, and, with the single exception of Antigua, adopted generally by the colonies.'*

*'This little colony being, from its geographical*

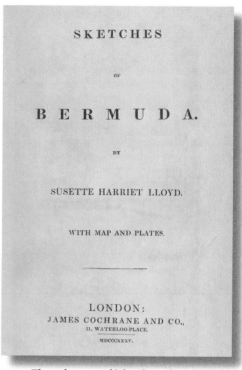

*The title page of 'Sketches of Bermuda', published in 1835.*

*A rather romanticized view of Flatts.*

*This view of Hamilton Harbour has obviously been embellished for the European travel book market.*

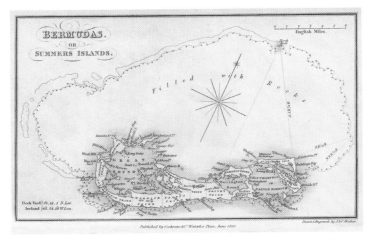

*Paynter Vale at Bailey's Bay in the typical style of the early 19th century, before the invention of photography*

*The Map of Bermuda shows the outlying reefs and the north of Bermuda 'Filled with Rocks'.*

situation, the key to our trans-atlantic possessions, naturally acquires considerable importance, while the singularity of its formation, the beauty of its scenery, and the variety of interest in its natural productions, seem to entitle it to a more distinct notice than it has yet received in the casual allusions of different writers.'

The 273-page 'Sketches of Bermuda' by Susette Harriet Lloyd includes beautifully engraved views of Hamilton, Flatts and Paynter Vale at Bailey's Bay, as well as a more detailed map of Bermuda than the one published a few years earlier by Richard Cotter in his book of the same title.

Do You Know …

## … About the First Bermuda Books?
## Part 3 – Col. Ferdinand Whittingham – 'Bermuda, A Colony, A Fortress and A Prison *or* Eighteen Months in the Somers Islands'

Col. Whittingham was stationed in Bermuda in 1855/56 and during his time on the island wrote a 298-page history of Bermuda and Bermudians from a garrison officer's perspective. In his preface he wrote:

*Bermuda possesses a three-fold claim to the attention of Britons, – as a colony, a fortress, and a prison.*

*As a colony; it claims interest from its remoteness, the beauty of its scenery, the salubrity of its climate; and also from its having been the earliest colonized of our islands in the western hemisphere.*

*As a naval and military fortress; its value, if not duly appreciated by us will, one day, certainly be so by the Americans.*

*Lastly, as a prison, Bermuda, as the receptacle of our worst convicts, must assuredly possess some degree of interest for every Briton who values the security of his life and property.*

Col. Whittingham's comments as to the value of Bermuda as a naval and military fortress to the Americans certainly proved correct, starting with World War I through to the end of the Cold War in the 1990s.

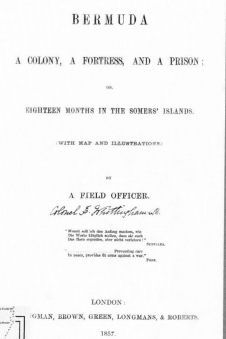

*The 1857 title page of 'Bermuda, A Colony, A Fortress and A Prison', signed by the author.*

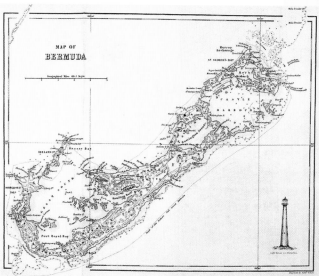

*This fold-out map of Bermuda is included in the book.*

'Bermuda, A Colony, A Fortress and A Prison' includes 8 interesting illustrations printed in duotone lithography based on photographs taken by H. Whittemore, a daguerreotypist who worked in North and South America, as well as the Caribbean, and known for the quality of his images, using a mirror for a reflector.

*Commissioner's House on Ireland Island.*

*'H.M.S. Nile' in Grassy Bay.*

*The Dockyard, Camber, Hulks and Barracks.*

*A View from Gibbs Hill.*

*St. George's from Barrack Hill.*

*Hamilton – West End of the Wharf.*

*An earlier Government House at Mount Langton showing the Governor in his impressive carriage.*

*The Summer Sleeping Tents of the Dockyard Troops with Col. Whittingham, his wife, daughter and her nanny.*

Do You Know …

# … Why William Perot created his famous Bermuda Postmaster Stamps?

William Bennet Perot, Postmaster of Hamilton from 1818 to 1862, spent much of his time in his garden, which is now Par-la-Ville Park. When he was required in his post office, his friend Mr. James Bell Heyl, the American proprietor of the Apothecaries Hall next door to the post office, would call Mr. Perot from the garden. Customers would then hand him their letter together with one penny for the postage.

For the convenience of others who wished to mail their letters after closing hours, Mr. Perot also provided a box outside the post office where people could leave their letters and pennies. Unfortunately, however, there were often more letters than pennies in the box, which was particularly annoying as those pennies were supposed to augment Mr. Perot's salary!

To solve the problem, Mr. Heyl suggested that his friend issue adhesive labels with a distinctive mark, such as his postmark. The idea was that letters could still be prepaid with cash during the day, however, anyone wishing to mail letters later, would buy stamps ahead of time and any unstamped letters found in the box would thereafter be treated as unpaid mail.

The Perot Post Office on Queen Street in Hamilton in the mid-1800's

To produce his 'stamps', Mr. Perot removed the date plugs from his postmark, leaving only HAMILTON BERMUDA and the year date. He then struck this postmark several times on a sheet of paper, wrote 'One Penny' above the year, signed each stamp below the year date and gummed the back of the paper. Little did he know that he was creating some of the greatest philatelic rarities in the world.

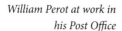

William Perot at work in his Post Office

It is uncertain when Mr. Perot made his first stamps, but it was probably not before 1848. The first stamps he made were struck in black ink, however, around June 1849 he changed the colour to red.

For nearly 50 years the Perot stamps were unknown, the first three examples being discovered in 1897 by Mr. Louis Mowbray of St. George's. He sent one, struck in red and dated 1854, to a London stamp dealer who did not consider it a proper stamp because it was not cancelled. Shortly after that Mr. Mowbray sold one of his stamps for £20. In 1898 another example was discovered, dated 1849 and struck in black. This example changed hands twelve years later for £150.

By 1957 a Perot stamp fetched £1,500 and more recently it is not unusual for one to change hands for over $100,000. Today the catalogue value of the eleven known examples, three of which are in the Royal Collection, ranges up to £275,000.

BERMUDA HISTORICAL SOCIETY

*William Bennet Perot, Postmaster of Hamilton from 1818 to 1862*

*The Bermuda Post Office has commemorated the Perot Postmaster Stamps on several occasions: In 1948 on the 100th Anniversary; on two stamps of the first Elizabethan definitive stamps issued in 1953, the 160th Anniversary in 2008; and more recently on the 200th Anniversary of the Bermuda Postal Service.*

Do You Know ...

# ... About Bermuda's First Postage Stamps, bad record keeping and unsuccessful speculators?

In early 1865 arrangements were made for the preparation of Bermuda's first three postage stamps - a One Penny stamp for local letters, a Six Penny stamp for letters sent to the British West Indies and British North America, as well as a One Shilling stamp for letters sent to the United Kingdom.

The stamps were printed by Thomas De La Rue and Company, using a portrait of Queen Victoria, engraved by Jean Ferdinand Joubert De la Ferte. Printed by the typographic process in sheets of 240, which were cut into four panes of 60 stamps each, the paper used was watermarked Crown CC and the stamps perforated 14.

Specimens of the new stamps were put on display at Bermuda's Public Library on August 1st, 1865, and following their arrival during the following month, the stamps were first used on September 25th, 1865.

Two Penny stamps were soon required and these arrived in Bermuda in March 1866. It was not until April 1872 that a Three Penny stamp was needed, following the reduction of the postage rate for letters sent to British North America. Production of these stamps was delayed by almost one year, due to the disagreement as to whether or not a portrait showing Queen Victoria as a widow should be used. The idea was dropped, however, due to the considerable costs involved, and the new stamps finally arrived in Bermuda in March of 1873.

Unfortunately record keeping at the Bermuda Post Office left much to be desired and the Three Penny stamps were used within one year, without new supplies having been ordered from England. As there were about 40,000 One Shilling stamps left, it was decided to surcharge some of those stamps 'Three Pence'. On February 21st, 1874, the Privy Council Minutes recorded 'The Council approve of the

issue of a portion of the redundant one shilling Postage Stamps in Store as three-penny stamps with a distinct crossing of "three" or "3d" in a different coloured ink'.

The overprinting was done by Sergeant Maddox of the Royal Engineers, with the Privy Council recording 'The Council order the payment of the charge of Sergeant Maddox for converting one shilling Postage Stamps into three penny stamps at 3/- per 1,000 stamps'. A total of 13,000 stamps were overprinted.

One year after the 'Three Penny' stamp fiasco, it was the stock of the One Penny stamp that was exhausted. So in 1875 it was again found necessary to overprint other stamps in Bermuda. As the One Penny stamps were in much greater demand than the Three Penny stamps, it was decided to have the Queen's Printer, Donald McPhee Lee, publisher of the *Royal Gazette*, carry out the printing of the larger quantity.

Half Penny, Two-and-a-Half Penny and Four Penny stamps were now required to cover various postage rates and these were issued in new designs. They were released in March 1880, November 1884 and sometime in 1880 respectively.

When reprinting various stamps, it was sometimes decided to change the colour of the stamps. Thus the Half Penny stamp was reprinted in green in November 1881, the Two Penny stamp in purple in June 1902, the Three Penny stamp in grey in January 1886 and the One Shilling stamp in brown in June 1892.

Finally, in 1900 it was decided to charge for the mailing of local newspapers which up to then were sent free of postage. As there were no stamps for the Farthing postage rate, an urgent request was made for Farthing stamps and it was decided to print One Shilling stamps in grey, and overprint them 'One Farthing'. The first shipment of 1,000 sheets (240,000 stamps) were all bought within 24 hours by speculators! Two more shipments of almost 1 million Farthing stamps were bought by collectors hoping for a quick return on their money, with the result that more than one hundred years later the Farthing stamps are hardly worth more than their face value.

When first on display at the Public Library in 1865, the *Royal Gazette* commented that the new stamps 'have been universally admired for elegance of design and neatness of execution'. For almost 150 years the admiration for these first postage stamps of Bermuda has never changed.

Do You Know …

# … How the world's largest Floating Dock came to Bermuda in 1869?

Bermuda's location as a half-way point of call between British colonies in the Western Atlantic and Great Britain itself, was considered an important location for a Dockyard, and especially a dock capable of lifting large war ships to avoid having to make the journey back to England or to the often ice-bound Dockyard at Halifax.

In the early1800's the idea of constructing such a dock of stone was seriously considered, however, because of the porous nature of Bermuda stone, this scheme was abandoned. Instead, ships were tilted to one side, allowing the scraping of the underwater section to clear it from barnacles etc., and make minor repairs.

It was Colonel Clarke, Director of Works of the Royal Navy, who suggested the construction of a Floating Dock according to the invention of Messrs. Campbell Johnstone and Co. and it was this shipyard that built *H.M. Floating Dock Bermuda* in North Woolwich, England. Employing as many as 1,400 workers, construction commenced in August 1866 and was completed in May, 1869.

The Floating Dock's overall length was 381 feet and overall breadth 124 feet, while the inside dimensions were 330 feet by 84 feet. Overall depth was 74 feet, inside depth 53 feet and the total weight, including the caissons, was 8,600 tons.

On June 24th, 1869, *H.M. Floating Dock Bermuda* began its 3,985 mile journey from England to Bermuda. Being towed by *HMS Northumberland* and *HMS Agincourt,* assisted by *HMS Warrior* and *HMS Black Prince,* with *HMS Terrible* guiding the stern, the epic journey took until July 27th.

*Floating Dock Bermuda under construction at the Campbell Johnstone*
*& Co. shipyard in North Woolwich in England.*

In April, 1870, *H.M. Floating Dock Bermuda* was moved into the Camber and served the Royal Navy until 1904. By then it was realized that *Bermuda* was too small for a new generation of war ships and sold to a German company. Having been partly dismantled, the Dock broke loose in a squall while being towed away and ended up at Spanish Point.

What remains 100 years later are just rusting iron plates and frames, with many Bermudians unaware that this was once the largest Floating Dock in the world, serving the Royal Navy well from 1870 to 1906.

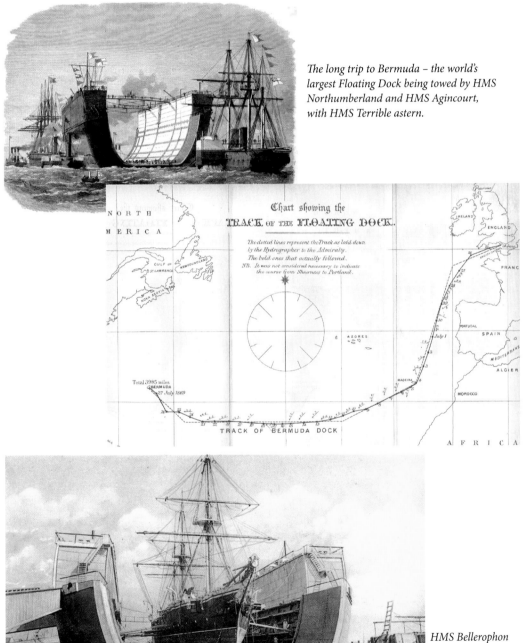

*The long trip to Bermuda – the world's largest Floating Dock being towed by HMS Northumberland and HMS Agincourt, with HMS Terrible astern.*

*HMS Bellerophon raised out of the water in Bermuda's Floating Dock at the Dockyard.*

Do You Know ...

# ... About Bermuda's Second Floating Dock AFD 1?

Bermuda's first Floating Dock had a lifting capacity of some 10,000 tons and served the Royal Navy from 1870 to 1906. The dimensions of warships increased substantially during that time and *HM Floating Dock Bermuda* was soon out of date.

In 1900 the British Admiralty placed the order for a new Bermuda Dock – *Admiralty Floating Dock 1* – with the firm of Swan, Hunter, Wigham & Richardson at Wallsend. 545 feet long and 126 feet wide, it was to have a lifting capacity of 17,500 tons.

When *ADF 1* was launched in February 1902, it was again the largest floating dock in the world. As a test, *ADF 1* had to lift the heavy battleship *HMS Sans Pareil* before being towed to Bermuda. Having successfully completed that task, *ADF 1* left Sheerness on June 16th, 1902, to be towed to Bermuda by two Dutch tugs – *Zwarte Zee* and *Oceaan*.

From Sheerness to the Azores the voyage took 21 days in mostly bad weather. After a four-day stop the voyage continued on to Bermuda, which, after encountering more bad weather and heavy cross seas, took 28 days.

On reaching Bermuda, the 6,500 ton floating dock was taken to the Great Sound and moored securely in Boss's Cove. Once the extension works at H.M. Dockyard were completed, *ADF 1* was placed in position on June 6th, 1905.

*Floating Dock AFD 1 moored in Boss's Cover awaiting the completion of the extension works at H.M. Dockyard*

*AFD 1 is finally moved to H.M. Dockyard*

*Playing cricket inside the Floating Dock! This photo shows the sheer size of AFD 1 – 100 feet between the sidewalls which were 53 feet high and 435 feet long*

*Here the Floating Dock is being listed to test the 56 divisions within the hull. The photographs show parts of the massive extension works which were built from 1902 to 1906 and changed the appearance of the vicinity of the Dockyard.*

*ADF 1 finally lifts it's first ship out of the water*

Do You Know …

# … That the game introduced to America from Bermuda in 1874 was actually Sphairistiké?

When Mary Ewing Outerbridge returned to her Staten Island home from a holiday in Bermuda in 1874, she had trouble getting through customs in New York. In her luggage the customs inspectors had found some curious objects – a long, narrow net, which did not look like a fishing net, and several implements with handles and webbed heads. Could they be rug beaters, butterfly catchers or perhaps snowshoes?

Miss Outerbridge explained that this was the equipment needed for a new outdoor game called Sphairistiké. A few weeks later this new game – clearly neither cricket nor baseball – was played at the Staten Island Cricket and Baseball Club. Across a net hung between two posts, gentlemen and ladies could be seen hitting a bouncing rubber ball with some sort of bat. Sphairistiké had come to America.

It was earlier in 1874, that Major Walter Wingfield had applied for a patent on "a new and improved portable court for playing the ancient game of tennis." A British officer and avid sportsman, Major Wingfield claimed that the new "portable court" constituted a new game, as the "ancient game of court tennis" was an indoor affair with complicated rules where a ball could bounce off all four walls and still be in play. Major Wingfield's game, on the other hand, was far simpler. All it required was a lawn, two posts and a net, and rackets to hit the ball with. It was much like badminton, with the important difference that in lawn tennis a rubber ball was used instead of a feathered "bird", making for a much more energetic contest.

A classical scholar, Major Wingfield based the name of his new game – Sphairistiké – on a Greek word meaning 'ball-playing'. For a popular game this was not exactly a great name. One wit wrote 'I hear that Major Wingfield intends bringing out a game with a Greek name. The name, I understand, will not exceed ten syllables, and may be easily mastered in six lessons'. Since the new game was clearly descended from court tennis, it quickly became known as lawn tennis and Sphairistiké was soon forgotten.

Right to the end of the nineteenth century few ladies ventured on the court in anything but lawn-sweeping skirts and large hats. Only slowly short skirts – that is, just above the ankle – and small hats were introduced. Tennis dress for men, on the other hand, started out on the casual side with knickers, tam'o-shanters, long trousers, colorful cravats, and bright blazers. Gradually, white became the favoured color, and by the end of the century fashionable players were seldom seen on the court in anything else, however, long white trousers and a white shirt was to prevail for another half century.

Other paraphernalia of the game – nets, balls, and rackets – evolved slowly during the early years of tennis. There was little change in the net, a little more in the ball and

*An early Bermuda tennis match at the Shore Hills Hotel at Ferry Reach,*
*now the Bermuda Institute of Ocean Sciences.*

most of all in the racket. In fact, the search has always been for a racket that would impart more speed to the ball with less effort, and this led to tighter stringing and metal frames. Yes, tennis is a great game and Major Wingfield and Mary Outerbridge deserve every tennis players' thanks.

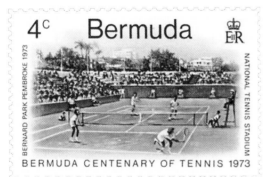

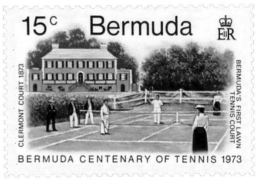

*In 1973 the Bermuda Post Office issued four stamps to commemorate the 100th Anniversary of Tennis in Bermuda.*

Do You Know …

# … About the making of a Princess? – Part 1

In the early 1880's Harley Trott, local merchant and head of the Trott & Cox steamship agency, proposed building a 200-room hotel on Pitts Bay. Because of the financial connection with the Quebec Steamship Company of New York, this proposal was rejected due to land holding regulations. Harley Trott then reduced the scale of the planned hotel to 70 rooms.

*Mr. Harley Trott*

*Princess Louise*

With H.R.H. Princess Louise, Duchess of Argyll and daughter of Queen Victoria, spending the winter of 1883 in Bermuda (her husband Lord Lorne was stationed in Ottawa as Governor-General of Canada), Harley Trott also came up with the name of the proposed new hotel – The Princess.

During 1884 the Princess was being built. When it opened on January 1st 1885 it was Bermuda's

*The Princess Hotel in the 19th century*

first waterfront hotel, built of wood to absorb the local humidity. It was also the first local hotel to offer hot and cold running water and was lighted with gas throughout. A.A. Jones, proprietor of Mansion House in Williamstown, Mass., was manager.

In 1889 and 1895 the Princess was enlarged to double of its original size, adding an enclosed veranda, 400 x 14 feet, with superb views of Hamilton Harbour. Nathan S. Howe had become manager of the hotel and at various times telephones, electricity and elevators were installed for the almost 300 guests that could now be accommodated. In 1897, two years after the enlargements, Harley Trott died, having not quite achieved his dream of a 200-room hotel on Pitts Bay.

## THE
## PRINCESS HOTEL,
### BERMUDA HOTEL COMPANY (Limited),
## HAMILTON, BERMUDA.

### SEASON 1885.

THIS New and Commodious house, delightfully situated on the shore of Hamilton Harbour, will be opened for the reception of guests on or about January 1st, 1885.

Its Architecture is that of a Southern hotel, the rooms being large and well ventilated, with beautiful Parlours, Dining-Rooms, Offices and Billiard-Rooms. The Hotel is fitted with seventy handsomely furnished bed-rooms, hot and cold, fresh and salt water baths, and is lighted with gas throughout. From the verandahs the views of the harbour, ocean, and surrounding country are unsurpassed.

Throughout the Islands there are over one hundred miles of the best carriage roads lined with mangroves and hedges of oleander, or running between moss-covered walls, dotted on all sides with white stone cottages, and gardens of tropical plants. A good livery is connected with the house.

The Cuisine will be under the entire supervision of the manager, and will be first-class in every respect.

Terms will be regulated by location of rooms, diagrams of which may be had and information obtained by addressing the Manager,

### A. A. JONES,
Hamilton, Bermuda.

ALSO PROPRIETOR OF **MANSION HOUSE, WILLIAMS-TOWN, MASS.**

### Or A. E. OUTERBRIDGE & Co.,
51 BROADWAY, NEW YORK.

*Announcing the Princess Hotel for the 1885 tourist season, this advertisement appeared in the Bermuda Almanack.*

Do You Know ...

# ... About the making of a Princess? – Part 2

By the beginning of the 20th century and fifteen years after the building of the original Princess Hotel, various additions had increased the capacity of the hotel to accommodate almost 300 guests. In both 1904 and 1905 further additions were completed and in 1907 several internal changes increased the number of bedrooms with private baths even further.

*The Princess circa 1900*

Following the death of manager Nathan Howe in 1907, his brother Frederick managed the hotel together with Leo Tworoger who would stay with the Princess as manager until 1940. In 1909 they added a new wing with 70 rooms at the northwest and the Princess could now accommodate 400 guests. Rooms were from $4 per day, $25 per week.

*In the 1920's...*

Not just rooms were added to the hotel, the Princess also built the first hotel swimming pool in Bermuda, provided a golf course for its guests, as well as facilities such as a popular grill room and a handsome ball room. The music provided by the hotel orchestra and the weekly dances became popular features not just for overseas guests, but Bermudians as well.

In 1924 a waterside colony club was added. The hotel now advertised itself as 'The Princess Hotel and Cardiff Point Cottages', offering the traveler of discrimination the ideal accommodation. Every requisite for convenience and comfort has been included – electric lights, elevator, room telephones, tiled swimming pool, grill room, spacious public rooms, tennis courts, golf course, saddle and driving livery, yacht fleet, and the Metropolitan Orchestra'.

Following the addition of the Adam Lounge in 1931 and a new western wing in 1932, the Princess promoted itself as the leading hotel in Bermuda – 'At every world-famed resort there is one hotel that leads. Such a hotel not only assures a congenial

*... and the 1930's*

atmosphere, but carries also the assurance of every expected luxury and comfort, as well as social diversions and sports facilities. There is such a hotel in Bermuda, and for over fifty years it has been the choice of the well-informed'.

During World War II the Princess Hotel was requisitioned by the Imperial Censorship Detachment sent to Bermuda to intercept and censor all trans-Atlantic mail between Europe and the United States. Following the war the Princess had become rather tatty and was sold to Englishman Sir Billy Butlin. Around 1960 American billionaire Daniel K. Ludwig planned the building of the huge Southampton Princess Hotel and, to show his goodwill, proposed to pur-

*A tatty Princess in 1945*

chase the run-down Hamilton Princess and completely renovate it. $9 million later, the Hamilton Princess reopened on April 1st 1964. Four years later the waterside cottages were removed and a 226-bed addition opened on the western side of the hotel.

*The Princess in the 1960's*

In 1980 Daniel Ludwig sold a 50% interest in the hotel to the British Lonrho Group who in turn sold the Princess Hotel as part of a seven property deal to Canadian Pacific Hotels in 1998. Together with Fairmont, they created the luxury brand that the Princess is today. Global Hospitality Investments purchased the Princess in 2007 and continue to operate the hotel as part of the Fairmont chain.

*The Fairmont Hamilton Princess today*

Do You Know …

# … About Fine Cuisine and Famous Guests at the Princess?

Since its opening, the Princess Hotel has been known for fine cuisine, professional service and genuine hospitality.

Leo Tworoger, assistant manager in 1890 and manager until 1940, took particular pride in the hotel's dining and entertainment facilities.

*Leo Tworoger and his team*

*The dining room around 1900…*

*…and a menu from the same period*

As word got out, celebrities started to appear at the Princess. Mark Twain, America's best known author and a regular at the hotel, would smoke cigars on the veranda while reciting poetry to groups of adoring fans. He was also known to frequent the billiard room. A statue of the famous author now resides in the main lobby of the hotel.

*Mark Train
in the billiard
room*

In 1920 HRH Prince of Wales, later King Edward VII, visited the hotel and 50 years later Prince Charles helped celebrate Bermuda's 250th Anniversary of Parliament at the Princess Hotel.

Over the years other famous guests included Ian Fleming, who is said to have used the fish tank lined Gazebo Bar as the motif in his novel Dr. No. Other celebrities included three-time World Heavyweight Champion Mohamed Ali and legendary soccer player Pele.

*HRH Prince Charles at the
Princess Hotel in 1970*

*Mohamed Ali at the entrance of
the Princess. At the left is Bodo von
Alvensleben who opened the hotel after its
renovations in the early 1960's*

*Famous soccer star, Edson Arantes Do
Nascimento, better known as Pele, in
the garden of the Princess. To his right
is then-manager Walter Sommer.*

Do You Know …

# … About Bermuda's First Postcards? – Part 1

Government-issued Postal Cards with pre-printed postal indicia were the forerunners of Picture Post Cards. They were first introduced in Austria in 1869, followed by other European countries and the United States in the early 1870s. Bermuda joined the Universal Postal Union in 1877, which required that Postal Cards be provided to the general public, however, it was three years before a supply of cards was printed locally in 1880. Actual postage stamps were applied to these cards when they were sold to the general public.

*A Postal Card sent by a tourist on March 12th 1886 from Hamilton to Cincinnati. The 1-1/2 pence postage is applied with actual postage stamps.*

By 1885 Postal Cards proved so popular that larger supplies were ordered from England for both local and overseas use. These had the image of the stamp printed on the card and were sold for the value of the imprinted stamp, making it an inexpensive way to communicate.

*Pre-printed with a ½ penny stamp for local use, this Postal Card was mailed from Devonshire North to St. George's on May 25th 1898.*

Around 1890 the first Picture Post Cards appeared in Europe and in 1893 at the Columbian Exposition in Chicago. These cards still had to be mailed at the letter rate postage as Governments tried to protect their privilege of issuing Postal Cards. By an Act of Congress of 1898, privately printed post cards could be mailed at the same postage rate as Government-issued Postal Cards in the U.S. They were called Private Mailing Cards.

Before this was allowed in Bermuda, one enterprising local came up with the idea of overprinting a picture on the back of Queen Victoria 1/2d Postal Cards. The only example that seems to have survived is a view of Hamilton from across the harbour in Warwick and is called 'View from Bellterre'. 'Bellterre' was a boarding house and tea room at the time, located next to what later became the Belmont Manor Hotel.

*Probably printed in the mid-1890s, this is a rare example of a privately overprinted Government-issued Postal Card. It is the first image of Bermuda on a Post Card.*

The earliest recorded Picture Post Card of Bermuda was mailed from St. George's to Hamilton on January 15th 1901. Sent by J. Golinsky, it was addressed to J. Jackson and concerned the steamship 'Carribee' which arrived two days late following the collision with another ship.

Up to 1907 the back of post cards was reserved for the address and postage stamp only, with any message from the sender restricted to the front of the card. It was for this reason that post cards printed prior to 1907 always left room for a message on the front of the card – either below or to the right of the design.

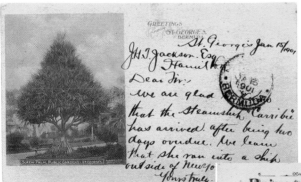

*The earliest recorded example of a Picture Postcard mailed in Bermuda. It was sent from St. George's to Hamilton on January 15th, 1901.*

*The back of the card was to be used only for the address and postage stamps. Any message had to be written on the front of the card. The ½ penny postage was paid with two Farthing stamps.*

Do You Know …

# … About Bermuda's First Postcards? – Part 2

When postcards were first introduced in Bermuda in 1901, most of them were printed monochrome in either black or dark green ink in the 'collotype' printing method. This process employed a glass plate with a gelatin surface which carried the image to be reproduced. The main supplier of these cards was the Albertype Company of Brooklyn, New York.

Other cards were printed from screened blocks by the 'surface printing' method, a process also called 'relief', 'typographic' or 'letter-press printing'. These cards can easily be identified because the image is broken up into screening dots, all of which are of the same colour intensity.

Shortly after these early postcards were published, various efforts were made to make Bermuda postcards more colourful – either by tinting black-and-white cards, using stencils to add colour, or printing by chromolithography, a method where the individual colour overlays were created by artists.

Weekly Steamships from New York.   Quebec S. S. Co., N. Y.
VIEW FROM GIBBS' HILL LIGHT-HOUSE, BERMUDA.

VIEW OF HAMILTON. BERMUDA.

BERMUDA POST CARD.

NORTH SHORE, BERMUDA.

VIEW FROM PRINCESS HOTEL, BERMUDA.

An innovative method of printing colour images was used by the Quebec Steamship Company starting in 1904 to illustrate their Bermuda travel brochures. Fortunately they used the same images to produce postcards for the use of their passengers. The method was based on photographing a scene with black-and-white film through colour filters representing the primary colours and the printing was done by the Attractive Advertising Company of Philadelphia.

Dr. Adolf Miethe was a German scientist who invented panchromatic film emulsions and in 1902 designed a 3-color camera to simultaneously expose an image through three colour filters. The resulting three black-and-white negative images represented the primary colours red, green and blue, required for colour printing.

The resulting pictures are the earliest colour photographic images of Bermuda, made more than 30 years before the invention of colour film, and it is indeed fortunate that one of these cameras was brought to Bermuda as early as 1904 to record these images.

A selection of Quebec Steamship Company postcards is shown on these pages.

*A Miethe three-colour camera*

Do You Know …

# … About Bermuda's First Postcards? – Part 3

The earliest postcards of Bermuda were printed monochrome in either black or dark green ink in the 'collotype' printing method. The process was popular because it reproduced photographic images most faithfully, however, it was limited to only a few hundred copies per gelatin plate, so impractical for the printing of large quantities.

To avoid this limitation of 'collotype' printing, postcards were soon printed from screened blocks by the 'relief' printing method. These cards can easily be identified because the image is broken up into screening dots, all of which are of the same colour intensity. While this method did not reproduce photographs as faithfully as the 'collotype' process, there was no limit as to how many copies could be printed from one printing block and therefore the cost of producing postcards was greatly reduced.

In an effort to make these black-and-white postcards more colourful, starting around 1904,

GOVERNMENT HOUSE, BERMUDA.

*Two examples of early black-and-white postcards printed from 'relief' blocks in the early 1900s.*

*As the back of the cards was reserved for the address and postage stamp only, these cards have a space for a message from the sender on the front.*

*Obviously these black-and-white postcards did not represent Bermuda very well and an effort was made to tint some of the cards with watercolour.*

ORDINANCE ISLAND AND CONVICT BAY, BERMUDA

Oct. 16, 05
Dear Elsie Best - greetings to you & your
mother.

BERMUDA.

FRONT STREET, WEST, BERMUDA.

DRILL AT PROSPECT CAMP, BERMUDA.

This is the only military card
I can procure    J.R.

*Three examples of hand tinted cards. This was not very pleasing when the subject matter was somewhat dark.*

some postcard publishers began to have their black & white postcards hand tinted to make them more appealing. Usually this was done by women, with each colourist responsible for a single hue which was applied in production line fashion. Sometimes stencils were used as a guide. Small companies would have one person apply all colours, but this tended to result in wider colour variations.

Tinting black-and-white cards that were printed with ink was obviously not easy using watercolour paint and the results were not terribly pleasing, especially dark areas of the photographic image.

As most of this work was done in Europe without any guidance as to the colour of Bermuda houses and roofs, Bermuda buildings often ended up with blue or red roofs, which did little to enhance the quality of these early hand tinted postcards.

Do You Know ...

# ... About Bermuda's First Postcards? – Part 4

Have you ever wondered how those 'fake' colours on early postcards were created? It was a complicated process called Chromolithography.

Invented by Alois Senefelder in Germany in 1798, lithography quickly became the preferred printing method for colour pictures. The process is based on the chemical repellence of oil and water, with designs drawn or painted with greasy ink or crayons on specially prepared limestones.

*Figure 1*

Multiple stones had to be used for each colour with the term Chromolithography specifically referring to lithographic prints produced in three or more colours from the 1880's through the First World War. Postcards relied heavily on black-and-white photographic images on which the primary colours were overprinted.

Although the optical mixing properties of primary colours was known for centuries, no colour separation techniques were available in lithography's early days and multiple hand drawn images were used to produce individual colours. See Figure 1.

Once individual stones were drawn, they were submitted to a cleaning in nitric acid to prevent any greasy matter from adhering to the areas not covered in lithographic ink. Test printings were then carried out on a hand press to check each colour, starting with the lightest and finishing with the most intense. See Figure 2.

When the proofs were judged to be o.k., they were given to the press operator as samples for the final printing done on a printing press. Individual sheets of paper were fed into the printing press by hand. See Figure 3.

After printing and drying, the sheets were cut into normal sized postcards, checked for quality, counted and packed for shipping. See Figure 4.

The Chromolithographic process

*Figure 2*

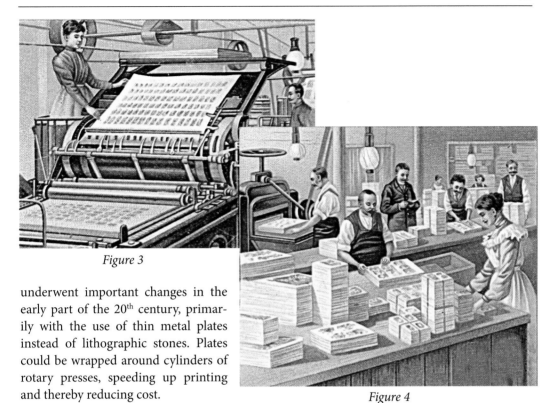

*Figure 3*

*Figure 4*

underwent important changes in the early part of the 20th century, primarily with the use of thin metal plates instead of lithographic stones. Plates could be wrapped around cylinders of rotary presses, speeding up printing and thereby reducing cost.

Further technical advances such as scanning and more recently digital photography have now changed the production of postcards completely since the days when postcards were first introduced in the early 1900's.

ENTERING TWO ROCK PASSAGE.                    S. Nelmes, The Tower, Hamilton, Bermuda.

*A typical Chromolithographic postcard of ca. 1902 published by S. Nelmes showing the S.S. Trinidad entering Two Rock Passage in the Great Sound.*

Do You Know …

# … Who was the Artist of these Hand Painted Postcards?

When collecting Bermuda postcards, one occasionally comes across hand painted cards, which usually include a poem.

Unfortunately none of these cards are dated, however, it would seem that they were created before the age of air travel, so perhaps the 1920s.

The cards are also unsigned, so this is an appeal to our readers. Can you help identify the artist?

The Voyage to Bermuda, so I've heard tell,
Is oftimes low'ry — sometimes bright,
But Mark Twain said that
"'Twas comin' thro' hell,
to get to heaven."
And he was right.

A little Angel fish am I,
Though I came not from the sky;
But in Bermuda you'll see me,
Which is next to Heaven, you see.

The trip to New York is merry and glad,
The ship doesn't roll
so no one is sad;
But when you anchor
in New York Bay,
You wish you were back
in Bermuda each day.

Do You Know …

# … Why Bermudians are nicknamed 'Onions'?

During the 1800s, onions, arrowroot, potatoes, celery, tomatoes, beets, carrots and later Easter Lilies were important export crops from Bermuda. Bermudian seamen became known as 'Onions' and Bermuda was referred to as 'The Onion Patch'.

*Packing Onions in Bermuda*

In 1875, 4,000 tons of onions were shipped to New York on the twice-monthly steamers and this continued until World War I when shipping almost came to a standstill.

This trade further declined after World War I when the United States imposed ever-higher import tariffs, and especially when farmers in Texas began selling their onions as 'Bermuda Onions'. Consequently the export of Bermuda onions dropped from 153,000 crates in 1914 to just 21,570 crates in 1923.

Texas – where the first Bermuda onion seeds were planted in 1898 – on the other hand started shipping Bermuda onions to northern markets already one year later. By 1907, over 1,000 railway carloads of onions were shipped, a figure that almost tripled two years later. Following World War I, shipments increased to around 7,000 carloads annually. Bermuda could no longer compete.

*A busy Front Street when local farmers delivered their crops*
*for shipment to New York*

*A Texas onion field against which Bermuda could not compete*

*A postcard mailing by the Bermuda Trade Development Board proved rather futile and could not reverse the decline of Bermuda's onion trade*

In the 1930s the Bermuda Trade Development Board tried to reverse the trend by mailing postcards to overseas recipients, advising them that:

*"It is the flavor of a genuine 'Bermuda' that is so different. Maybe it is the Sunshine and Sea Breezes down in beautiful Bermuda or some magic in the soil that is responsible, but whatever it is the flavor tells the difference immediately. Be careful then to always look for the crate as shown in this picture: that is how genuine 'Bermudas' are shipped. See that it is marked 'from Bermuda Islands' and you'll know you are getting the real thing."*

Today onions are Texas' leading vegetable crop worth around $350 million annually to the Texas economy.

*A Bermuda postcard captioned "Blessed is the man who comes to Bermuda and is tempted to eat a sweet onion instead of a forbidden apple"*

Do You Know …

## … About J.J. Bushell, M.B.E. – publisher, musician and educator?

John James Bushell was born in Weymouth, England, in 1872 and came to Bermuda at age 15 with his Bermudian mother and British father. He was one of the original students of Isaac Pitman, the inventor of the shorthand system. When in Bermuda he brought the first typewriter to the island and it would seem that publishing was an early interest of his.

In 1895 J.J. Bushell published 'A Business Directory and Commercial Advertiser of the Islands of Bermuda'. This later became 'Bushell's Handbook', which he published until 1939. By 1901 the 1895 edition of 16 pages developed into 'All About Bermuda. Bushell's Handbook. History, Guide, Directory and Compendium of Information on the Bermudas. A Tourist Guide', totaling 160 pages of information plus a 54 page Advertising Directory. By 1911 'All About Bermuda' was still the same size, however, it was now simply called 'Bushell's Handbook'. With the growth of tourism and colour printing becoming more accessible, J.J. Bushell in 1926 wrote 'A little story about Bermuda written for those who desire a brief and

*John J. Bushell*

accurate narrative'. This attractive booklet includes 49 images of Bermuda in colour, and was published by the Bermuda Furnishing and Supply Company.

*In 1926 J.J. Bushell published 'Bermuda' with the subtitle 'A little story about Bermuda written for those who desire a brief and accurate narrative'. The 49 colour images of Bermuda included this interesting aerial view of Hamilton taken from one of the small floatplanes operating sight-seeing flights in Bermuda.*

Meanwhile 'Bushell's Handbook' became 'Picturesque Bermuda in Picture, Prose and Poetry' in 1927 and in 1932 'Picturesque Bermuda. The land that is different!' which included three Road Maps and 40 pages of photographs. From 1935 to 1939 – the final edition – the now 254 page book got a new cover treatment showing Sir George Somers and a map of Bermuda.

In 1906 the very active J.J. Bushell opened the 'Bermuda Tourist Association', Bermuda's first tourist bureau. The following year he merged his growing printing business with the 'Colonist' newspaper, becoming manager of both. From 1911 to 1920 he was managing editor of the 'Colonist'. After the 'Royal Gazette' and 'Colonist' were merged in 1921, J.J. Bushell became manager, however, he resigned in 1924 to join the 'Mid-Ocean News'.

In addition to his interest in printing, publishing and tourism, J.J. Bushell was instrumental in starting the Bermuda Chamber of Commerce in 1907, was organist of the Wesleyan Centenary Church and secretary-treasurer of both Saltus Grammar School and the Bermuda High School for Girls. He died in 1953 at the age of 81.

*The changing covers of 'Bushell's Handbook' from 1901 to 1939.*

Do You Know ...

*A Cedar Candlestick ...*

*... Cedar Box ...*

*... Snake Shoe ...*

*... Paper Knifes ...*

*... Beaker and Cup*

# ... About the Boer War Prisoners that were brought to Bermuda?

Over 4,600 Boer War prisoners were brought to Bermuda in 1901 and encamped on the islands in the Great Sound – about 450 on Burt's Island, 1,000 on Darrell's Island, 1,350 on Hawkins' Island, 240 on Hinson's Island, 750 on Morgan's Island and 800 on Tucker's Island.

To relieve the monotony of camp life, some prisoners took up carving – mostly cedar wood, but sometimes also beef bone, slate and silver. The carvers on Burt's Island were the most enterprising and established an industrial association, which sent finished items to various gift shops in Hamilton for sale to tourists.

*An intricately carved Picture Frame in the shape of a palette*

Cedar walking sticks were the most common carvings and usually inscribed 'BERMUDA', 'POW' and '1901' or '1902'. Other cedar items included boxes, picture frames, paper knifes, napkin rings and cups. A popular toy were small shoes with a slide on the top which, when opened, released a snake. This was perhaps a sign of defiance by the Boer prisoners.

Miniature pocket knives were the rarest of the curios produced by the Boers. These were made out of 6 penny and one shilling coins, showing part of the portrait of Queen Victoria on the handle.

*Miniature Pocket Knifes made from
6 penny and one shilling coins*

*A Cedar Napkin Ring carved
by a Boer prisoner*

In accordance with the terms signed at the conclusion of the war, all Boer prisoners were to be returned to South Africa as soon as they signed a Declaration of Allegiance to the British Crown, specifically King Edward VII.

Effectively the Boer prisoners were now split into three groups – those who could afford to pay for their transportation were free to leave, with some going to the United States. The second, and largest group, waited for British ships to take them back to South Africa. And finally there were the 'Irreconcilables' who refuses to sign the Declaration of Allegiance. They were told to 'shift for yourselves'.

Eventually the 'Irreconcilables' were moved from the islands to Hamilton. Some found jobs as carpenters and farmers. One set up shop on East Broadway and continued to carve souvenirs for tourists. Two got married to Bermudian girls, but all of them had left Bermuda by about 1917.

*A Cedar Jewellery Box …*

*… Book Box …*

*… and Snake Walking Stick carved from one piece of cedar wood.
Details of the Walking Stick are shown above*

Do You Know …

Boer Prisoners of War landing at Bermuda.

# … How the Boer War Prisoners communicated to and from Bermuda?

The story of the 4,619 Boer prisoners-of-war who were brought to Bermuda in 1901, held on seven islands in the Great Sound, and largely repatriated upon the cessation of hostilities in South Africa in June 1902, is well documented. While in Bermuda, these prisoners were allowed to write and receive as many letters as they wished, and it is estimated that an average of 5,000 were written each week.

Some letters to Boer prisoners were so badly addressed, it is surprising that they ever reached their destination. This cover, addressed in phonetic English, was mailed in Natal on 3 November 1901 and marked 'Try Bermuda'. It arrived in Hamilton on 27 December.

Postmasters were soon elected by the prisoners of each camp – Burt's, Darrell's, Hawkins', Hinson's, Morgan's, Port's and Tucker's Islands – and a censorship department set up by British military authorities on Port's Island. While writing material was distributed free of charge, postage stamps and postal cards had to be purchased.

All outgoing and incoming mail was censored by up to four censors on Port's Island, each one using a different hand stamp to indicate censorship. One can assume that the unnumbered first censor mark was made for the first censor who was able to cope with the mail from and to the first prisoners who arrived in January 1901. However, when 3,000 prisoners had arrived by late-1901, it was obviously necessary to employ more censors and create individual marks for each one.

Much of the incoming mail from South Africa was not censored on arrival in Bermuda, as it had already been dealt with at its source; those that were censored in Bermuda, were stamped with one of the four censor marks. There are just a few incoming covers that were stamped with all four censor marks and one can assume that this was done as a favour to some prisoners who were shrewd enough to appreciate the future philatelic value of such envelopes.

While incoming and outgoing Boer prisoner-of-war mail exists in roughly equal numbers, examples of local mail to and from the prisoners are very scarce. The few known examples were sent to members of the Boer Relief Committee and to the crafts shops that sold the cedar souvenirs carved by the Boers.

*One of the few letters that shows all four censor marks used in Bermuda. It was sent from Natal on 27 September 1901 and arrived in Bermuda on 5 November.*

*Sent to Mrs. Herman Recht, a member of the Boer Relief Committee and owner of a gift shop that sold many of the souvenirs produced by the Boers, this cover was hand painted, and shows one of the bell tents in which the prisoners lived.*

Do You Know …

# … About the ill-fated Swastika – the last Bermuda-built Pilot Boat?

On July 28th, 1910 the last Bermuda-built pilot boat was launched at Burchell's Cove in St. David's. On August 2nd the Royal Gazette commented on the launch:

### LAUNCH AT St DAVID'S ISLAND

#### "Swastika" Takes the Water

#### INTERESTING CEREMONY

The stocks on which the boat was built were several hundred feet to the South and West of the spot selected for the launching. Some few months since a specially constructed cradle was built underneath the boat, and on this, with the aid of hydraulic jacks, rollers, skids, etc. and 'willing hands' the boat was moved across the land, up the public road leading to the pier, and then on to the western side of the Point.

The steamer Daisy left Market Wharf at 12 noon, filled with passengers, all bound for the launching. As she pawed through the Narrows into Smith's Island Sound a pretty picture presented itself. The flag staffs on the hills were decorated with flags and the pilot boats MicMac, Secret and Guard lay at their moorings tastefully decorated.

The steamer Daisy leaves the wharf and backs down to the boat and her cradle and a line is made fast; the Daisy then goes gently ahead, taking the strain gradually. One o'clock is approaching, all are getting nervous; just as the hour arrives the pistol is fired, Mrs. A. Cassidy Fox breaks the bottle of champagne across the boat's stern saying "I christen thee Swastika". Pilot Fox pulls the string and a black pigeon escaped from a cage under the bowsprit. At 1.46 Swastika glides gracefully on to the water with a fair wind. She floats high and compels the admiration of all. "She is a beauty" is heard from all directions.

After shaking hands with Pilot Fox and wishing him success once more, the company disperses but not before each one had expressed his delight at having been present at the Swastika's launch. Here are several meanings to the yacht's name, viz. "Four winds", "Good luck", etc. but the most appropriate one is "Fortunate".

*The Swastika four months before its launch in Burchall's cove, St. David's*

*The postcard Marriott Morris sent to his son in Philadelphia*

According to Jane Downing of the Bermuda Maritime Museum, the Swastika met an untimely end when she was abandoned at sea by her crew. Perhaps her name was a bad omen, even though the Swastika was launched years before that iconic Hindu symbol representing the cycle of birth, suffering, death and rebirth was made infamous in Nazi Germany. The other curious fact is that, according to Jane Downing, no plans or photographs are known to exist of the *Swastika*. That is until I looked through some old Bermuda postcards of mine and found a rather unusual cyanotype card showing a boat being built. On closer examination I realized that the image was taken in March 1910 in St. David's by the famous photographer Marriott C. Morris. Although Marriott Morris is best known for his fabulous black-and-white images, he also made cyanotypes, a process invented in the 1840's using a combination of ferricyanide and ferric ammonium citrate. This mildly photosensitive solution is then applied to paper and allowed to dry in a dark place. A positive image is then produced by exposing it to sunlight through a negative and afterwards rinsing away the unexposed solution with running water, leaving the non-water-soluble Prussian blue. This is what gives cyanotypes their typical blue colour. Marriott Morris, from a wealthy Philadelphia family related to Bermuda's Perot family, visited Bermuda on several occasions. When here in March 1910, he made the postcard showing the *Swastika* four months before being launched and mailed it to his 11-year-old son Elliston Perot Morris. This was his message:

Hamilton Bermuda 3/28.1910
Dear Elliston
   When we went to St. Davids' Island the other day, it was most interesting to see this boat being built by some colored men. You can see them working on the deck. It was a long way from the water, and I do not see how they are going to launch it. Someone told me it is to be a pilot boat. Yesterday Mother and I went to the fort at Prospect, and attended the soldiers church, sitting among the redcoated Englishmen. Mr. Godet and de Grail and Martin went up there with us.
   We find we can stay till the 4th of next month and hope to be home at that day. I sent Miss Ely a cable message about it. This is the last time I can write to You, before we get home. 'Thy loving father. These blue pictures were all taken by me since we came here.

   Obviously Marriott Morris made several cyanotypes on that trip and it would be great to discover some of the others.

Do You Know …

# … About Bermuda's connection with the invention of Wireless Broadcasting?

Canadian-born Reginald Fessenden was the first man in history to send wireless broadcasts of voice and music and was also the inventor of the sonic depth finder and various submarine signaling devices. In total he held over 500 patents.

*Reginald Fessenden,*
*Inventor of wireless broadcasting*

Born in 1866, Fessenden spent much of his childhood in Ontario, where he excelled in mathematics and, at the age of 10, watched Alexander Graham Bell demonstrate the telephone. He closely studied Bell's work and dreamed of transmitting the human voice without wires. During his brilliant academic career at Trinity College School in Ontario, financial problems forced the not quite 18-year-old to look for a job. Through his uncle Cortez he heard about a position as Headmaster of a small private school in Bermuda, a position he quickly accepted.

It was the Whitney Institute and apart from being Headmaster, Reginald Fessenden was also the only teacher!

On his first day in Bermuda, young Reginald met Helen May Trott, daughter of businessman/farmer Thaddeus Trott. For the first and only time in his life he fell in love. One Saturday, after helping the Trott family crate a huge order of tomatoes for shipment to New York, Mr. Trott asked Reginald point blank: "Have you made up your mind yet, young fellow, how you intend supporting my daughter?"

"I can't, sir," replied Reginald, "But I intend working with Mr. Edison in New York while I learn all I can about electricity. Edison pays a good wage, twenty or thirty dollars a month, enough to live on." "Electricity?" replied Mr. Trott. "You mean there's a future in that?" "Well, not exactly," fumbled Reginald. "You see I must know a lot about electricity before I get anywhere at sending voice without wires. Then you could talk from Bermuda to New York and you would know the prices for onions, tomatoes and potatoes from hour to hour."

It obviously took a lot of convincing for Mr. Trott to agree that such a hairbrained young man should marry his favourite daughter Helen. But finally it was decided that after barely two years in Bermuda, and not yet twenty years old, Reginald would go to New York and, armed with letters of introduction to all the important people Mr. Trott knew in New York, seek an interview with Mr. Edison.

After several frustrating weeks trying to get the interview with Mr. Edison, Reginald Fessenden was finally hired by the Thomas Edison Machine Works and furthered his research in wireless communication. Although few of his colleagues shared his view that broadcasting voices was possible, Reginald Fessenden was able to transmit radio's first voice message from an island in the Potomac River, to a friend about a kilometer away. Radio broadcasting was born.

*Reginald Fessenden, In his laboratory*

While the inventor of the wireless telegraph, Guglielmo Marconi, believed that sound waves were created by a spark causing a whiplash effect, Fessenden argued that sound waves continuously rippled outward, like water when a stone has been dropped into it. In 1906 he was finally able to demonstrate radio's real potential. On Christmas Eve, he broadcast the first programme and wireless operators on ships in the Atlantic heard him play "O Holy Night" on the violin and wish them a Merry Christmas.

During World War I, Reginald Fessenden invented a wireless system for submarine communication, devices to detect enemy artillery and locate enemy submarines, as well as the 'fathometer', an ocean depth device. Unfortunately Reginald Fessenden spent much of his time with legal suits, defending his own place in history as the inventor of radio broadcasting. In 1928, he was finally awarded $500,000 in his long-standing patent dispute.

That year, aged 62 and in failing health, Fessenden and his wife Helen returned to Bermuda where he died on July 22, 1932. He is buried at St. Marks Church in Smith's Parish. His grave is inscribed:

BY HIS GENIUS DISTANT LANDS CONVERSE AND MEN SAIL UNAFRAID UPON THE DEEP

Today the Fessenden-Trott Scholarships administered by the Bank of Bermuda HSBC remind us of Professor Reginald Aubrey Fessenden and his Bermudian wife, Helen May Trott.

*Reginald Fessenden's grave in Bermuda.*

Do You Know …

# … Where the 1914 Silent-Movie Classic 'Neptune's Daughter' was filmed?

Produced by Universal Studios at the then huge cost of $35,000, 'Neptune's Daughter' was filmed in Bermuda – largely at Crystal Cave and the Hamilton Princess Hotel where the company stayed. Underwater scenes were filmed at the Bermuda Biological Station, then located on Agar's Island.

In 'Neptune's Daughter' the daughter of King Neptune, starring Annette Kellermann, determines to avenge the death of her sister who was caught in a fishing net, however, she falls in love with the king upon whom she planned to take her revenge. 'Neptune's Daughter' was based on Annette Kellermann's idea of "a water fantasy movie with beautiful mermaids in King Neptune's garden together with a good love story."

*A 1914 postcard showing Annette Kellermann as a mermaid and Allen Walker as the sea witch at the Crystal Cave.*

Fortunately for Universal Studios 'Neptune's Daughter' proved a huge success and grossed $1,000,000, largely due to the popularity of Annette Kellermann, an Australian swimmer with many records to her credit. In 1906 she performed her vaudeville aquatic act in Chicago, Boston and New York where she earned $1,250 a week! Unfortunately the Boston police was not amused by her one piece, skirtless bathing suit, and promptly arrested her. This did not diminish her popularity and established her as a fighter for women's rights.

In 'Neptune's Daughter' Annette Kellermann performed her own stunts, including an 18-meter dive into a pool containing five crocodiles. Her sister recalled that although "she was in and out almost before her back was wet … for months after she would wake up screaming". Unfortunately while filming a fight scene on Agar's Island, the glass front of the tank gave way, slightly injuring Miss Kellermann and seriously cutting the villain. Technically a mermaid, her outfit as Neptune's Daughter consisted of nothing but a body stocking and a flowing wig, giving the impression of total nudity!

Judged the 'perfect woman' from 10,000 contestants in the USA – though she quipped "from the neck down" – Annette Kellermann was a strong advocate of swimming for physical health, fitness and beauty and in 1918 published "Physical Beauty and how to Keep It" and the autobiographical "How to Swim". She died in 1975 at the age of 89 in Australia. A film of her life, "Million Dollar Mermaid", starring Esther Williams, appeared in 1952.

*The movie poster for 'Neptune's Daughter'.*

*A poster showing Annette Kellerman as "The Perfect Woman" in "Neptune's Daughter', comparing her measurements to those of the Venus de Milo and the Roman goddess Diana.*

*The one piece bathing suit that got Annette Kellermann arrested in Boston.*

Do You Know …

# … That German Prisoners of War were interned in Bermuda during World War I? – Part 1

While there were approximately 4,600 Boer prisoners in Bermuda during the Boer War, there were never more than about 60 Germans interned here during World War I.

The majority of the internees were officers and crew members of the following ships: *Bermudian, Cayo Soto, Caribbean, Leda, Kent, Chaleur, David Baird* and *Vesterland*, with the largest group of 38 coming from the *Leda*. Although some had served in German military services previously, none of the internees were actually military prisoners.

*German Prisoners of War on Ports Island in 1918. Photo: National Archives of Canada.*

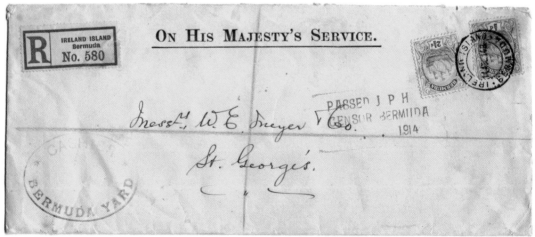

*This registered letter sent by the Royal Navy in Ireland Island to the W.E. Meyer Boat Yard in St. George's is an example of the cooperation between the Royal Navy and a German-owned company after the outbreak of World War I. It was mailed on August 14th, 1914, and censored in Hamilton by John P. Hand.*

Some local German residents were also arrested, as was an ex-Boer War prisoner of German birth who refused to swear the oath of allegiance to the British Crown and never left Bermuda after the Boer War. Other Germans were spared this fate, including Heinrich Friesenbruch who had asthma, Wilhelm Frederick Sondy due to his old age, and Captain William E. Meyer, whose company W.E. Meyer & Co. was considered loyal to the British Crown.

*A letter sent by German Prisoner of War Erich Röhr in 1917 to a newspaper in Hamburg, Germany. The letter was checked by Assistant Provost Marshall Captain Charles P. Pitt (top right corner), endorsed 'OK RB' by Miss R.S.G. Butterfield, the interpreter for German, and finally censored by the Chief Censor Major William Robert Winter using his handstamp and initials WRW. Erich Röhr was a cook and 23 years old at the time of his internment in Bermuda.*

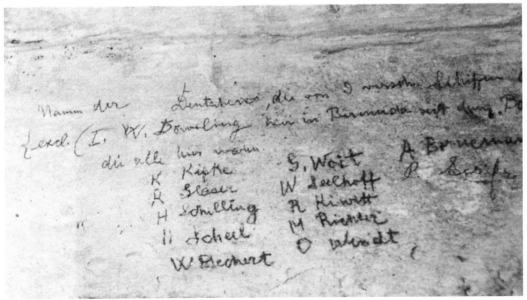

*The German prisoners interned at Fort Albert in St. George's left behind a permanent record of their confinement.*

Do You Know ...

*A selection of cedar jewellery boxes made by German Prisoners of War
on Ports Island during World War I.*

# ... That German Prisoners of War were interned in Bermuda during World War I? – Part 2

While most of the German POWs were held on Ports Island in the Great Sound, some opted to transfer to Fort Albert in St. George's where they wrote their names on the fort's walls, leaving a permanent record of their confinement. Others were sent to the St. George's detention barracks for breaches of discipline, including the 'unruly' ex-Boer War prisoner William Dowelling. Also imprisoned in St. George's Barracks were 38 Germans brought to Bermuda from Belize in 1916.

The prisoners on Ports Island did their own cooking and cultivated vegetable gardens, grew potatoes, raised chickens and rabbits, as well as a couple of pigs. Until the United States entered the war in 1917, some of the prisoners made a variety of cedar items including walking sticks, napkin rings, picture frames and boxes of various sizes. Usually these items were carved 'G.P.O.W.' – German Prisoner of War. When World War I ended there were 48 German prisoners in Bermuda who were repatriated back to Germany.

For more information about German Prisoners of War in Bermuda see Andrew Bermingham's 'German Internees in Bermuda during the First World War' in the Bermuda Journal of Archaeology and Maritime History Vol. 4 1992.

*A pair of cedar napkin rings carved G.P.o.W. Bermuda.*

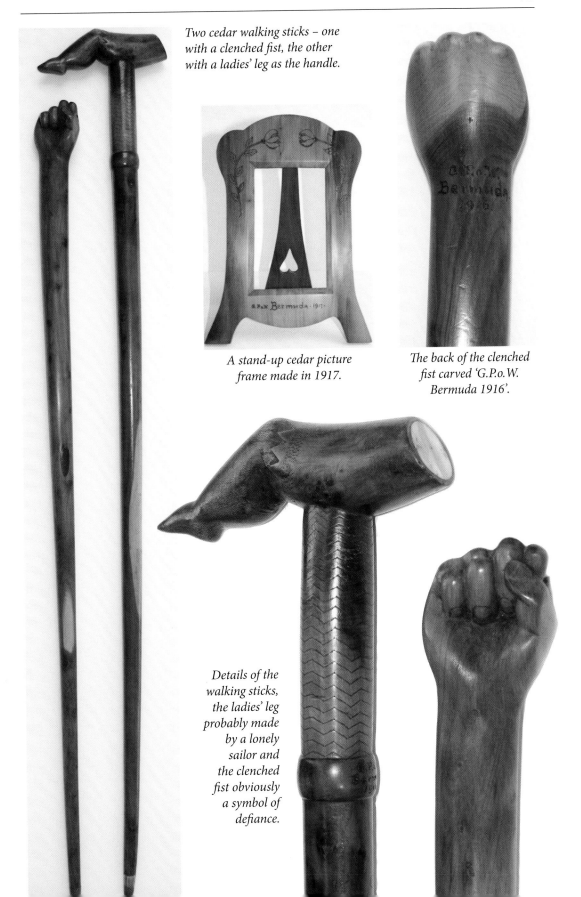

*Two cedar walking sticks – one with a clenched fist, the other with a ladies' leg as the handle.*

*A stand-up cedar picture frame made in 1917.*

*The back of the clenched fist carved 'G.P.o.W. Bermuda 1916'.*

*Details of the walking sticks, the ladies' leg probably made by a lonely sailor and the clenched fist obviously a symbol of defiance.*

Do You Know ...

# ... About Bermuda's remarkable sisters – Ethel and Catherine Tucker?

Ethel and Kate, born in 1874 and 1879 respectively, were two of the eight children of Robert Richard Jennings Tucker and Leonora Mary Tucker of The Lane House in Paget, now Tamarisk Hall. While raising a large family, their artistic mother found time to design wallpaper and paint Christmas cards and that talent was obviously picked up by young Ethel and Kate.

*Catherine and Ethel Tucker*

When Miss Eliza D. Williams' school was established on Reid Street in Hamilton, Ethel was keen to take art lessons from an American lady teaching at the school. She was also encouraged by Mr. James B. Heyl, who hired her to illuminate the margins of photograph albums he was selling at his drug store at Heyl's Corner. Getting one shilling per page, Ethel's artistic talent was already paying off handsomely.

In her late teens Ethel was off to New York to study art at the New York School of Applied Design for Women and after returning home for a holiday, took her younger sister Kate back to New York to study painting too. While studying, the Tucker sisters worked at a variety of jobs and eventually spent eleven years in New York – designing art embroideries, working for an interior decorating studio on Fifth Avenue, and teaching art themselves.

Before World War I they decided to return home and branch out on their own, opening a souvenir shop on Queen Street, in what is now the Bermuda Library. Their beautiful water-colour paintings of Bermuda soon became so popular with tourists that they decided to have colour reproductions made. Already very much a business woman, Kate travelled to Germany to get in touch with a well-known colour printer, and soon Ethel and Kate found themselves in the picture postcard business.

In 1915 they opened The Little Green Shop, now the Perot Post Office, and this became their shop for more than 40 years, selling original paintings, reproductions and postcards, as well as a wide range of souvenirs. After World War I it was impossible to get colour printing done in Germany and Ethel and Kate negotiated with J. Salmon Ltd., the colour printers in Kent, England, who would print their postcards, notelets, playing cards and calendars for rest of the 20th century. Their postcards alone numbered 100 different.

When the Prince of Wales – later King Edward VIII and after his abdication Duke of Windsor – came to Bermuda in 1921, he purchased 20 paintings by the Tucker sisters. His mother, Queen Mary, was obviously impressed with the paintings and ordered some for herself. These are now part of the Queen's famous collection of water-colour paintings.

Another enterprise that Ethel and Kate operated was the Little Green Door Tea Shoppe in Barrs Bay, just outside Hamilton. Here they hosted Mark Twain, Eugene O'Neill and Rudyard Kipling, among many other luminaries. Novels and short stories of the period often featured the Little Green Door as the setting for a social rendezvous or romantic interlude. On a masthead outside the Little Green Door they proudly flew their own 'House Flag' – yellow with a black teapot, signaling 'Tea is ready'. Unfortunately the flag violated a regulation forbidding advertising signs against the skyline.

When a zealous new Chief of Police arrived in Bermuda in 1934, he decided to enforce several flagrantly violated regulations, including the removal of Ethel and Kate's flag which had been flying outside the Little Green Door for 25 years. So when a police constable reluctantly approached Miss Kate and ordered her to remove the flag, she flatly refused. When taken to court, the Tucker sisters argued that the Furness Withy Line flew a flag with an 'F' and the Princess Hotel used one with a 'P'. The court, however, ruled that these were 'house flags' whereas the tea pot was advertising, and ordered the flag to be removed within one month.

*All illustrations are from 'Glimpses of Bermuda' by Ethel and Catherine Tucker*

Ethel and Kate were far from defeated. They flew the tea pot flag for exactly one more month and then raised a new yellow flag bearing a large 'T'. As expected the police again intervened, whereupon Kate innocently claimed that the 'T' had nothing to do with advertising. The 'T' stood for Tucker, not Tea, and was her house flag. Out-maneuvered, the Chief of Police gave up and the flag continued to fly until the Little Green Door closed in 1938. Dubbed the 'Bermuda Tea Party', the story made international headlines.

Because of Bermuda's short tourist season in the early 20th century, lasting from Christmas to just after Easter, the Tucker sisters opened other Little Green Doors and painted at Muskoka Lakes in Canada, Lake Placid in the Adirondacks, and in Florida. They also opened an antique shop on Burnaby Hill with a branch at the Castle Harbour Hotel.

By breaking through the rigid conventions of their childhood, these two outstanding Bermudian ladies were certainly far ahead of their time, yet their love of Bermuda is summed up in a quotation from their book 'Glimpses of Bermuda': Nobody hurries in Bermuda. "Tomorrow comes soon enough, today is delightful, and one is still enjoying yesterday."

Do You Know ...

# ... About the first U.S. Military Base in Bermuda?

In October 1917, after the United States entered the First World War, the first of many convoys of American Submarine Chasers anchored in Hamilton Harbour on their way to France. In March 1918 White's Island in Hamilton Harbour was leased to the United States Government as a stores depot and a number of buildings were built as warehouses. Officially this was the U.S. Navy's Naval Base No. 24.

Isle of White and City of Hamilton.                    S. Nelmes, The Tower, Hamilton, Bermuda.

*The Isle of White, better known as White's Island, in Hamilton Harbour before it became the U.S. Navy's Naval Base No. 24.*

*The only letter mailed at the Isle of White Navy Base that is known to have survived. It was marked 'Sailors Mail Foreign Service' and was mailed on March 22, 1919.*

*Sent by an officer stationed on USS Tallahassee, this postcard was mailed in Bermuda on March 16, 1919.*

*A postcard sent by a sailor on USS Leonidas on May 8, 1919. It is interesting that 'BERMUDA' and 'B.W.I.' is part of the ship's postmark.*

In the early days of Naval Base No. 24, the USS Prometheus – the U.S. Navy's largest repair ship – was stationed in Bermuda to service the many ships crossing the Atlantic for France. She was first replaced by USS Alert, and later USS Tallahassee, a submarine tender.

Another US Navy vessel that came to Bermuda regularly was the USS Leonidas, a tender capable of supplying two squadrons of submarine chasers. After the war she escorted convoys of homeward bound submarine chasers from the Mediterranean via the Azores and Bermuda back to New York.

To meet the needs of the hundreds of US sailors who were in Bermuda regularly, a group of about twenty American ladies living in Bermuda formed 'The American Navy Club' in December 1917. Rooms were loaned free of charge by the Bermuda Drug Company and opened on Christmas Day with Bermuda's Governor Sir James Willcocks as guest of honour.

Countless US sailors were entertained at 'The American Navy Club'. There was always a well-cooked meal being served; there were weekly dances held; and there was a writing room well-stocked with Bermuda postcards for those wanting to write home.

With the end of World War I and most of the ships having returned to the US, the American flag was lowered on White's Island in May 1919 and Naval Base No. 24 ceased to exist.

Do You Know …

# … Who first saw Bermuda from the Air?

It was during May of 1919 that an American astronomical expedition, en route to the South Atlantic to observe a solar eclipse, was forced to call at Bermuda for engine repairs. On board the 'S.S. Elinor' was Professor David Todd of Amherst College, head of the expedition and friend of Bermuda's Governor, General Sir James Willcocks. When the two met, General Willcocks mentioned his ambition to be the first to take a bids-eye view of Bermuda. After all, his official title designated him 'Governor of and <u>over</u> the Somers Isles', and it would be only appropriate for him to make the first ascent.

It so happened that a seaplane formed part of the expedition's equipment, and it was quickly decided to make the Governor's wish come true. On the following day, Thursday, May 22nd, 1919, the Curtiss N-9H 'Jenny' was lowered from the 'S.S. Elinor', and amidst great excitement His Excellency the Governor was taken in a rowboat from the Royal Bermuda Yacht Club to the seaplane. General Willcocks then made history – he became the first person to see Bermuda from above.

*General Sir James Willcocks*

With Ensign G.L. Richard at the controls, the seaplane headed from Hamilton Harbour through Two-Rock Passage to Spanish Point, and across the Great Sound to H.M. Dockyard. After circling Ireland Island, the plane once again returned to Hamilton Harbour. In describing his first flight, General Willcocks said: "I knew that Bermuda was a beautiful spot, but I never knew how truly beautiful are the many islands when looked at from above: the whole scene reminded me of the Arabian Nights".

During the twenty-minute flight the Governor dropped "A Message of Goodwill to the People of Bermuda". This letter was contained in a canvas-covered package attached to a wooden float. It was found two days later by a boy, Dudley Butterfield, swimming off Point Shares.

*General Willcocks climbing aboard the Curtiss 'Jenny' in Hamilton Harbour.*

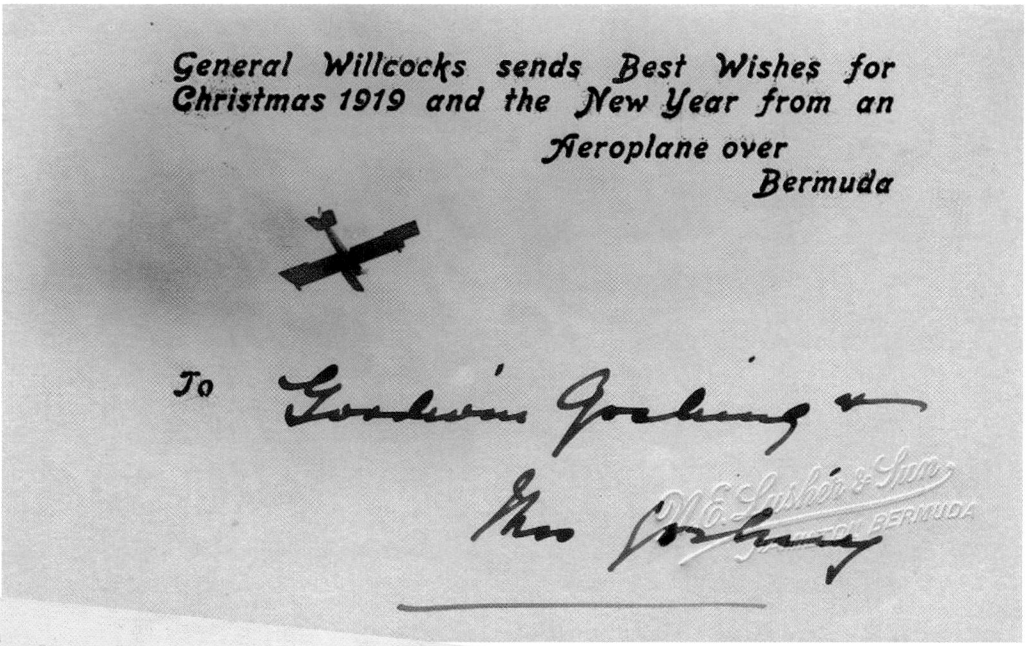

General Willcocks sends Best Wishes for Christmas 1919 and the New Year from an Aeroplane over Bermuda

To *Goodwin Gosling &*

*Mrs Gosling*

*This postcard shows the Curtiss 'Jenny' while flying over Bermuda. It was used by General Willcocks as his Christmas card in 1919.*

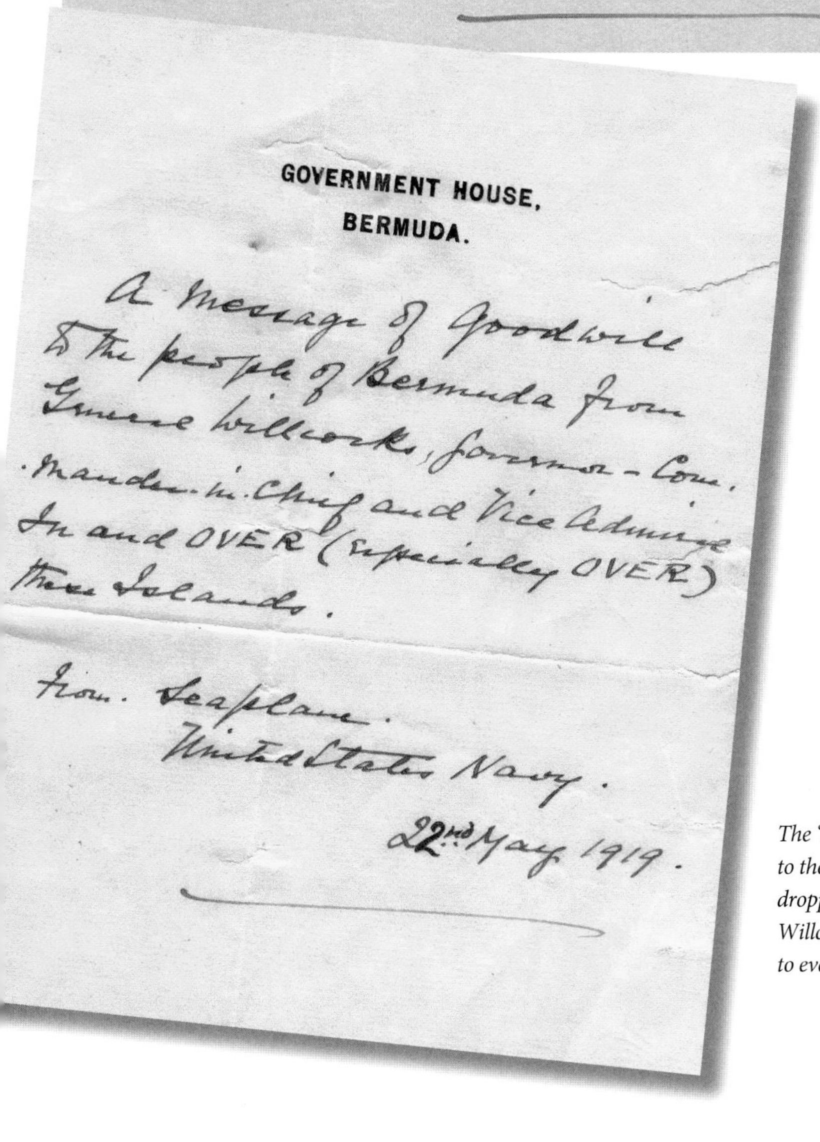

GOVERNMENT HOUSE, BERMUDA.

A Message of Goodwill to the people of Bermuda from General Willcocks, Governor - Commander-in-Chief and Vice Admiral In and OVER (especially OVER) these Islands.

From. Seaplane. United States Navy. 22nd May 1919.

*The 'Message of Goodwill to the people of Bermuda' dropped by Governor Sir James Willcocks from the first plane to ever fly above Bermuda.*

Do You Know …

# … About Bermuda's first Commemorative Stamps – 18 of them!

On August 1st, 1620, the Legislative Assembly of Bermuda met for the first time. With the exception of the British Parliament, Bermuda's Legislative Assembly is the oldest representative institution within the British Commonwealth.

To celebrate the 300th Anniversary, it was proposed to issue a set of Commemorative postage stamps – a first in Bermuda's history and also one of the first such Commemorative issues by a British colony.

In early March 1920, the following notice was published in local newspapers:

*"The local Government has under consideration the issue of special postage stamps in two values, one penny and two pence halfpenny, to commemorate the Tercentenary of the Establishment of Parliamentary Institutions in Bermuda, which is to be celebrated in August next.*

*"Suggestions are invited for the appropriate design for the proposed stamps. Suggestions may be either accompanied by a rough sketch or design or may indicate in general terms the form which it is proposed the design should take. What is required is not a design but a suggestion which can be worked up into a design.*

*"As time for the preparation of the stamps is short, it is particularly requested that any suggestions forwarded may reach the Colonial Secretary on or before Saturday the 13th instant."*

*The nine stamps based on the design suggested by Bermuda's Governor, General Sir James Willcocks …*

*... and the nine stamps designed by local architect H.J. Dale, showing the Sword of State, the Speaker's Gavel, the Coat of Arms and the 'Sea Venture', as requested by the Legislative Assembly of Bermuda.*

With the approval of the Executive Council, the Governor, General Sir James Willcocks, forwarded his own suggestion for a design to the Crown Agents, with the request that the printers proceed with the printing of the stamps. An essay was submitted by De La Rue & Co. on May 18th.

Unaware that the Governor had already taken this action, the Legislative Assembly informed the Governor on June 9th that they had decided to commemorate the Tercentenary by an issue of nine stamps from 1/4d to 1/-. With this turn of events, Governor Willcocks informed the Assembly of what had already been done and submitted the De La Rue essay.

The Assembly was not happy with the design and felt that it should include emblems appropriate to the Tercentenary – the Sword of State, the Speaker's Gavel, the Coat of Arms and the 'Sea Venture' – and hired local architect H.J. Dale to prepare a new design.

It would have been simple to proceed with the new design, however, as time was running short and the new design would not have been ready until the following year, the Assembly now decided that two series should be printed – one of each design in nine denominations each. Thus Bermuda's first Commemorative Stamp issue ended up being 18 stamps!

In total 3,531,240 stamps were printed, with both sets remaining on sale until the end of 1924. Remainders were destroyed in 1925 – in some cases more than two-thirds of the entire printing of certain values.

The apparent lack of interest in this first Commemorative Stamp issue of Bermuda, and the fact that all remainders were destroyed, makes these stamps very collectable today.

Do You Know …

# …What Leonard Bascombe hauled up with his mooring line on October 15th, 1928?

Eighty years ago the *Graf Zeppelin* was considered the finest airship ever built. 776 feet in length, 100 feet in diameter and with a volume of 3,700,000 cubic feet, she made 590 flights covering more than one million miles, carrying over 13,000 passengers.

Her first flight was on September 18th, 1928, and less than four weeks later, on October 11th, she started the first transatlantic crossing from Friedrichshafen near Lake Constance in Germany. Bound for Lakehurst, New Jersey, the *Graf Zeppelin* had 61 people on board – 40 crew members, 20 passengers and a 19-year-old stowaway.

As the airship headed towards the Atlantic, heavy storms were reported and it was decided to take a more southerly course by way of the Azores, rather than the planned route via Newfoundland. The trip was not without difficulties, however, as the airship suffered potentially serious damage to its port tail fin on the third day of the flight when a large section of the linen covering was ripped loose while passing through a mid-ocean squall line. With the engines stopped, the ship's riggers did their best to tie down the torn fabric to the framework and sew blankets to the ship's envelope while attempting to not fall to the raging seas below. Fortunately the riggers finished just before the engines were restarted after the airship had dropped to within a couple of hundred feet of the ocean's surface.

Meanwhile cables arriving in Bermuda from New York, stated that the *Graf Zeppelin* had broken the 'port horizontal' and local rumour had it that the dirigible was heading directly to Bermuda to get within reach of assistance should she have to make a forced landing. Then came the news that the airship had made her own repairs and that a more northerly route would be taken to Lakehurst, bypassing Bermuda. This was followed by a wireless transmission from the steamer *Larcomo*, giving the position of the Graf Zeppelin as 62 miles east of St. David's.

As the airship was battling 35 miles an hour headwinds, her speed dropped to only 22 miles an hour and she took a course more closely to Bermuda. During the early evening of Sunday, October 14th, the *Graf Zeppelin* passed directly over St. George's and at 1,000 feet could be seen from stem to stern.

During the passage over St. George's a package was dropped from the airship. This information was radioed to New York and a cable sent to the Royal Gazette & Colonist Daily requesting that the package be found if at all possible. Due to the high winds and the probability that the package was carried out to sea, there was little expectation that it would ever be found. That is until Leonard Bascombe hauled up his mooring line!

Attached was a thoroughly soaked small bag containing a number of postcards with the request that they be taken to the Post Office and forwarded by ship to New York. This was done by the Postmaster of St. George's who, even though the postage stamps had soaked off the postcards, dried them and applied both the St. George's date stamp of October 15th 1928, as well as the AIR MAIL SERVICE BERMUDA handstamp which was used three-and-a-half years earlier when the airship *Los Angeles* visited Bermuda.

It is uncertain just how many postcards were in that soaked bag Leonard Bascombe hauled up in St. George's Harbour. It is known, however, that about half a dozen have survived and that they are very much sought after by collectors of Bermuda postal history, Zeppelin mail, as well as aerophilately. So if you find one of them in your attic, it could be worth several thousand dollars!

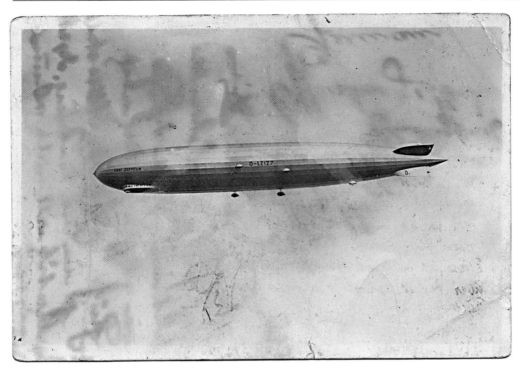

*One of the postcards dropped into St. George's Harbour. It shows the Graf Zeppelin, as well as some of the writing from another postcard.*

*The address side of another dropped postcard.
Where the postage stamp had soaked off, the Postmaster
of St. George's applied his date stamp, and further down the AIR MAIL
SERVICE BERMUDA handstamp. On arrival in New York the date stamp of October 18th was applied,
as well as the instructional marking POSTAGE STAMP REMOVED BEFORE RECEIPT AT THE
N.Y.P.O.FOR.SEC. (New York Post Office Foreign Section).*

Do You Know …

# … About Sir Trounsell Gilbert – a Bermudian in Zanzibar?

Born in Bermuda in 1888 and educated at Saltus Grammar School, Joseph Trounsell Gilbert won a Bermuda Rhodes Scholarship in 1907 and studied at Brasenose College, Oxford University.

In 1912 he was appointed Assistant Collector in the British protectorate of Zanzibar in East Africa. After being called to the English Bar in 1914, he returned to Zanzibar as Acting Magistrate, became Assistant Secretary one year later and was promoted to First Assistant Chief Secretary in 1928, a post he held until his retirement in 1933. At the Colonial Office Conference in London in 1930 he represented Zanzibar and was invested with the Order of the Brilliant Star of Zanzibar.

*Sir Trounsell Gilbert as Chief Justice of Bermuda*

After his return to Bermuda in 1933, Trounsell Gilbert practiced law until 1937; was Attorney General from 1938 to 1952; a Member of the Executive Council and Legislative Council; and Chief Justice of Bermuda from 1952 until his retirement in 1958. He received an M.B.E. in 1927; an O.B.E. in 1933; a C.B.E. in 1949 and Knighthood in 1955. He died in 1979.

Now a semi-autonomous part of Tanzania, Zanzibar is an archipelago made up of Zanzibar and Pemba Islands, totaling approximately 650 square miles. A centre of the centuries-old eastern slave trade, Zanzibar formally became a British protectorate in 1890 and, acquiescing to British demands, finally ended the slave trade in 1897. From 1913 – a year after Trounsell Gilbert's arrival – until independence in 1963, the British appointed 'Residents' (essentially Governors) of Zanzibar.

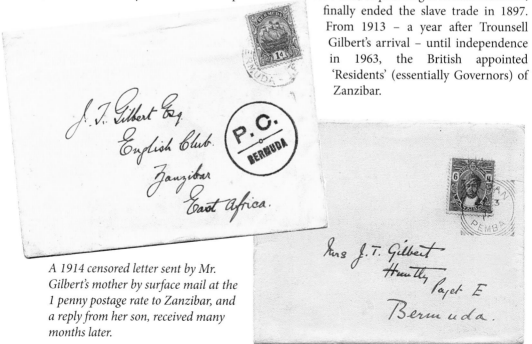

*A 1914 censored letter sent by Mr. Gilbert's mother by surface mail at the 1 penny postage rate to Zanzibar, and a reply from her son, received many months later.*

Communications between these two outposts of the British Empire – Bermuda in the western Atlantic and Zanzibar in the Indian Ocean – was certainly tedious in the early 20th century. Letters from Bermuda to Zanzibar, sent via London, typically took a couple of months. The same was of course true in reverse and it was therefore many months before a response to a letter was received back in Bermuda. As all surface mail letters only cost 1 penny in postage throughout the British Empire, one could hardly complain about delivery times.

*A letter sent by surface mail to London and airmail from London to Zanzibar at the cost of 8 pence*

The situation finally improved in 1931 when letters could be sent via Imperial Airways by air from London to Nairobi and a local airline from Nairobi to Zanzibar. Letters from London now took less than one week to reach Zanzibar, which obviously came at a price as the cost of an airmail letter from London to Zanzibar was 7 pence, which, with the 1 penny surface rate from Bermuda, made for a total of 8 pence postage.

Although Zanzibar's airfield at the time was just a long green field with a weather balloon and a telephone, the airfield manager's job description was anything but simple. Not only was he Aviation Control Officer, he was also Immigration and Emigration Officer, Customs Officer, Health and Medical Officer, as well as 'Postmaster Extraordinary'!

Sir Trounsell's career was certainly an impressive one – from Head Boy at Saltus Grammar School and Rhodes Scholar at Oxford University, to being a key administrator of a British protectorate in East Africa, and finally Chief Justice back home in Bermuda.

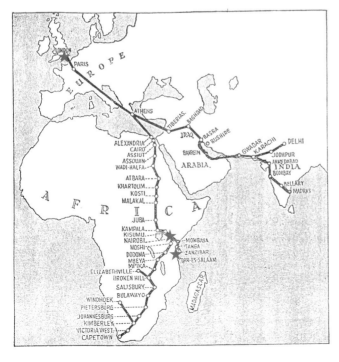

*The first airmail route from London to Capetown, with the additional route to Zanzibar in the Indian Ocean*

Do You Know …

## … That per mile, the Bermuda Railway was the most expensive railway ever built? – Part 1

Getting about Bermuda has always been somewhat of a problem, due mainly to the extremely elongated geography of the many coral islands. With public transportation limited to a few ferries plying their trade between the islands, and horse-drawn carriages providing a rather uncomfortable and unreliable service along the narrow and twisting roads, Bermuda's land transportation problems were the cause of many debates during the late 19th century.

In 1875, keeping the islands' defences and other military considerations in mind, the Governor, Major General John Henry Lefroy, asked London to provide a light railway for Bermuda. This project was eventually abandoned because the causeway was considered too narrow and flimsy to accommodate the tracks. By 1904 the Bermuda Electric Light, Power and Traction Company, Limited was formed and granted a concession to not only provide electric power, but also a transportation system. At the same time a number of buses appeared on the colony's roads and the company decided to concentrate their efforts on light and power services.

The buses, meanwhile, operating whatever route they wished, without timetables and unregulated by Government, caused much resentment amongst both Bermudians and tourists. Several petitions were soon presented to the Legislature, urging the prohibition of all automobiles. One of these petitions, presented by 112 American guests of the Princess and Hamilton Hotels, drafted by Woodrow Wilson and signed by Mark Twain, undoubtedly carried much weight. Two months later, the 1908 Motor Car Act temporarily ended the career of the automobile, and Bermudians

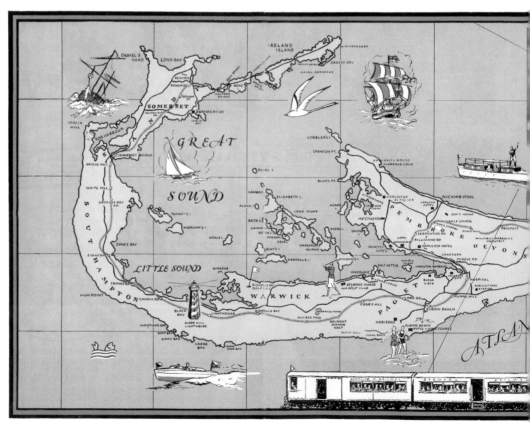

and tourists alike had to again rely on horse carriages, bicycles, and their own feet for transportation.

Against the backdrop of banned buses and the introduction of electricity, the Bermuda Trolley Company made its appearance in 1910. Proposing an electrified tramway system that would link Hamilton to both St. George's and Ireland Island, the scheme was devised by Canadian railway mogul Sir William Mackenzie. At a cost of £200,000, the system was to basically follow the existing roads, which were to be widened, thereby minimizing the impact on land holdings. Opposition to the proposed trolley system was swift. Arguing that the technology was inappropriate, spoiling the quiet life which drew tourists to the island; and above all against the "audacity" of a company organized in Quebec calling itself a Bermuda company, the opponents soon defeated the proposal.

In 1912, a Government-sponsored report on the inland transportation problems recommended that a railway, built along its own right-of-way, would "best serve the demand for rapid and frequent communication between the extremities of the island." No action followed this report until 1924, when a proposal was finally made to build such a railway. By then there were some 1,000 carriages and 7,000 bicycles on Bermuda's roads. The population was about 32,000. Opponents of the scheme promptly submitted a proposal to form a motor bus system and the debate centered around the relative merits of both schemes. Although a variety of vehicles such as ambulances, fire engines, tractors, and mobile stone crushers were allowed on Bermuda's roads, various petitions for motor cars were consistently refused - in 1928 a petition from doctors, in 1929 a petition from the Post Office to import four mail vans, and in 1931 a petition from the Governor to import and use an automobile.

The petition to build a railway was finally approved, and Bermuda Traction Limited was formed. After untold delays in purchasing land for right-of-ways, construction commenced in 1926. Difficulties were immediately encountered because of the rolling contour of Bermuda, and the many road and water crossings that had to be spanned. In all, some 10% of the track was spanned with 22 steel bridges and 34 timber trestles. The 22.5 miles of track formed a single line, divided into 15 sections, with 14 two-lane loop stations allowing "up trains" to pass "down trains," and 44 scheduled stops.

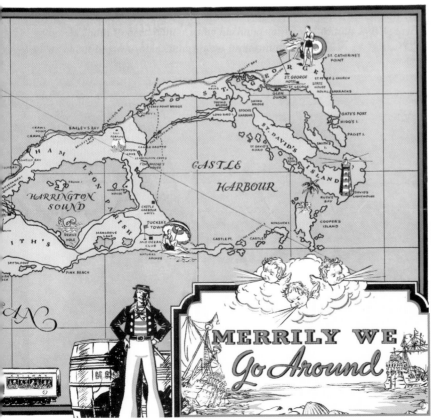

The route of the Bermuda Railway is indicated in red on this Railway Map of the early 1930s. The railway's primary rolling stock consisted of 6 Motor Coaches, 2 Motor Freight Locomotives, 2 Double Motor Truck Locomotives, 6 1st Class 'Pullman' Chair Cars, 6 Covered Passenger Cars and 2 Trailer Box Cars.

Do You Know …

## … That per mile, the Bermuda Railway was the most expensive railway ever built? – Part 2

The Hamilton-Somerset section was completed first, the maiden voyage taking place on Hallowe'en in 1931, when 150 local dignitaries, including the Governor, boarded the train in Hamilton for a trip to Somerset. On an upgrade, the train stalled and half the passengers had to walk up the hill – the beginning of a rather checkered career! When the Hamilton – St. George's section was completed in December 1931, costs had reached £1 million, making it the most expensive railway, per mile, ever built. At 2.5 miles per year, the rate of construction was also the slowest ever achieved.

During World War II, Bermuda's railway was heavily used for both passenger and material transport, especially during the building of the U.S. Naval Base. During 1945 alone, 1,600,000 passengers travelled on the railway – the peak usage of the system – and still the company did not show a profit. Without proper maintenance and replacement of rolling stock, concern soon mounted as to the safety of the entire system, especially the wooden trestle bridges, which were showing signs of rot.

While the restricted use of motor vehicles by the various armed forces was permitted during the war, many Bermudians pressed for the general use of motor cars once hostilities terminated in 1945. Anticipating a great reduction in traffic and faced with massive repair bills, the privately-owned Bermuda Railway Company sold out to the Bermuda Government in January 1946 for £115,000. During 1947 the passenger count fell to 662,000. Rather than spend the estimated $850,000 on repairs, the Government decided to sell the Bermuda railway – lock, stock and barrel – to the Government of British Guiana. On 31 December 1947, the last train left for Somerset and dismantling began. Eight months later, the Bermuda Railway, having carried 14 million passengers in its 17-year history, sailed for British Guiana, where it continued to operate between Georgetown and New Amsterdam.

Meanwhile, Bermuda fell under the spell of the motor car and despite the assurances of the proponents of private cars that they would never number more than 500, there are now around 25,000 private cars on Bermuda's 20.5 square miles. And as the population has increased to some 68,000, the total number of vehicles, including motorized cycles, has reached well over 50,000! All

*The Bermuda Railway made up for any shortcomings by providing passengers the most spectacular vistas of Bermuda. Here, the train is seen on a trestle at Bailey's Bay.*

that is left of the Bermuda Railway now is the Railway Trail – a scenic right-of-way for both visitors and Bermudians to enjoy and remind us of the "good old days".

More information about the Bermuda Railway can be found in Colin Pomeroy's 'The Bermuda Railway. Gone – But Not Forgotten!" available in Bermuda book stores.

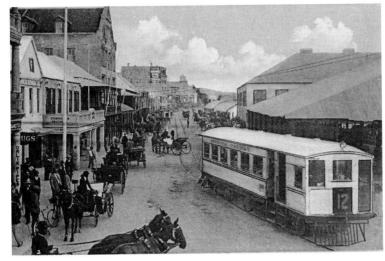

*One of the six 20-ton 120 horse power petrol-engined passenger cars on Front Street. Seating capacity was for 16 first class and 26 second class passengers. This postcard was published by the Photogelatine Engraving Co. of Ottawa.*

*A later model 29-ton 300 horse power passenger car is shown on this postcard published by Walter Rutherford and A.J. Gorham. There are no cars or trucks on the road, just horse-and-carriages, some pushbikes and the 'Queen of Bermuda' at the dock on Front Street.*

*This early aerial colour photograph of Hamilton by Walter Rutherford shows a Bermuda Railway passenger car on Front Street, next to the freight shed. At that time most freight was still brought to Bermuda on sailing vessels.*

Do You Know …

# … That in 1929 a proposal was made to build a Floating Airport between New York and Bermuda?

By 1929 more than 400,000 passengers were traveling the world by air. While many saw a great potential for rapid air transportation of mail, cargo, and passengers, the reality was that no airplane was able to fly economically beyond a 500-mile range at that time. Although Charles Lindbergh had crossed the Atlantic two years earlier, doing so with a load of passengers and cargo was still in the distant future.

Edward Armstrong, an engineer who specialized in aviation design and construction, and an authority on transoceanic flight, was convinced that "in any type plane, now developed or proposed, equipped for ocean flying, it will require almost an engineering miracle to extend useful payload to a thousand miles. Fundamentals of design and performance fix very definite limits to economic flight distance – distances that fall very short of spanning either the Atlantic or Pacific."

Armstrong's solution to the problem: a seadrome that would be a "floating landing deck" – an anchored airport and refueling station. It would ride high above the waves, moored at one end so as to trail the wind and be big enough to permit the landing and takeoff of most planes. Supported by tubular columns 70 feet or more above the surface, waves would pass through underneath, with the columns themselves terminating in ballast tanks 100 feet below the surface.

In 1926 Armstrong incorporated the Seadrome Development Company and, with the enthusiasm created by Lindbergh's flight, raised enough money to move his research out of the laboratory. By early 1929 he envisioned service between America and Europe, using eight seadromes, with planes leaving hourly in both directions and a flying time of 30 hours. To demonstrate the practicality of the scheme, Armstrong planned to put into place one seadrome connecting New York City with Bermuda.

*An artists impression of the proposed floating airport to be anchored half way between New York and Bermuda.*

Flying time for each leg would be approximately three hours. Passenger service would be scheduled only during daylight hours, but a night mail plane would deliver the New York newspapers for sale in Bermuda in the morning. For those wishing an overnight experience on the seadrome, there would be a hotel with 40 guest rooms, and during the day a café, a lounge, and other facilities would serve up to 350 people. 1,100 feet long and 340 feet wide, the New York-to-Bermuda seadrome was estimated to weigh about 50,000 tons.

In the summer of 1929, Armstrong built a 35 feet long scale model and anchored it in the Choptauk River near Cambridge, Maryland. He tested it in a variety of wind, wave, and current conditions and concluded that a full-scale seadrome could survive 280-mile-per-hour winds and waves up to 144 feet high. He announced that construction of a full-size seadrome would begin in the Chesapeake in December, and the finished structure would be towed to sea the following summer.

Unfortunately his announcement coincided with the New York Times headline PRICES OF STOCKS CRASH IN HEAVY LIQUIDATION, TOTAL DROP OF BILLIONS. It was the beginning of the Great Depression and potential investors found nothing reassuring about seadromes or the stock market. It was also the end of the scheme to build a seadrome between New York and Bermuda.

*'Pilot', the first plane to fly to Bermuda, at Murray's Anchorage after a night spent at sea 60 miles north of Bermuda.*

The Bermuda Trade Development Board had earlier offered a $25,000 prize for the first direct flight to Bermuda, however, aeronautical experts considered it too hazardous and the prize offer was withdrawn. Still an attempt was made a few months after the collapse of the seadrome scheme – on April 1st 1930 of all dates – by a Stinson monoplane equipped with pontoons and called *'Pilot'*, piloted by William Alexander with Lewis Yancey as navigator and Zeh Bouck as radio operator, to fly non-stop to Bermuda.

Sixty miles north of Bermuda *'Pilot'* unfortunately ran out of fuel and had to land at sea. After refueling the following morning, *'Pilot'* finally made it to Murray's Anchorage – the first plane to (almost) fly non-stop to Bermuda. Having been tossed around for a night on the open Atlantic, and after receiving a $1,000 cheque each from the Trade Development Board at a special dinner at the Hamilton Princess, the three aviators were in no mood to attempt a return flight to New York. Instead, they and *'Pilot'* returned to New York on the steamship *'Arcadian'*.

Do You Know …

# … That the Flying Boat 'Cavalier' was assembled in Bermuda?

In 1937, Imperial Airways and Pan American World Airways started a New York to Bermuda air service with Imperial Airways using their Empire flying boat *Cavalier*. With a range of about 1500 km, *Cavalier* was unable to fly to Bermuda and was shipped here by sea and assembled in Bermuda.

Built by Short Brothers of Rochester in England, the S.23 *Cavalier* had a wingspan of 35 meters, a length of 27 meters, an empty weight of 10.9 tons and a loaded weight of 18.4 tons. *Cavalier* was powered by four Bristol Pegasus engines, each providing 920 horse power. Cruising speed was 165 mph and maximum speed was 200 mph. *Cavalier* had two decks: an upper deck for the flight crew and mail, and a lower deck with luxury passenger accommodations.

*The fuselage of Cavalier is being lowered into the water at Bermuda's Dockyard …*

*… and towed to Darrell's Island for assembly.*

After being dismantled by Short and Imperial Airways engineers at the Rochester factory, *Cavalier* was shipped to Bermuda in 21 crates aboard the *RMS Lochkatrine*. The largest crate – 90 x 19 x 12 feet – containing the fuselage, was the largest crate ever to be shipped from London and was used for many years as both a work shop and club room. After unloading at Bermuda's Dockyard, the fuselage was towed to Darrell's Island where *Cavalier* was re-assembled under the supervision of Imperial Airways engineer Len Turnhill.

On 18th February 1937 *Cavalier* took to the air once again and on 8th June made the first of two inaugural flights to New York. After flying twice per week between Bermuda and New York, disaster struck on 19th January 1939 when, less than half way between Port Washington and Bermuda, icing of the carburetors forced *Cavalier* to land on the water. After sending an S.O.S. signal and first reporting 'okay' after landing on the storm-tossed waves, ten minutes later came the one-word message 'sinking' and then silence.

Of the thirteen people aboard the *Cavalier*, three died in the icy waters of the North Atlantic and ten were rescued by the tanker *Esso Baytown* and taken to New York. The loss of the *Cavalier* meant the end of Imperial Airways pre-war involvement on the Bermuda to New York route.

More information on Bermuda's flying boats can be found in Colin A. Pomeroy's 'The Flying Boats of Bermuda'.

*Assembly is almost complete inside the hanger on Darrell's Island.*

*Cavalier is finally back in the water outside Bermuda's first Airport on Darrell's Island . . .*

*. . . and off to New York.*

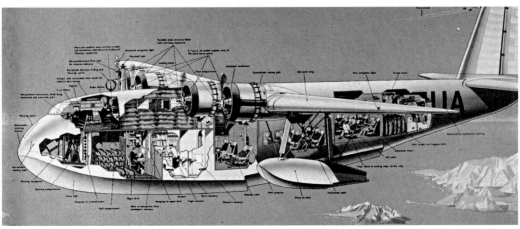

*The interior layout of Imperial Airways 'C' Class flying boats.*

Do You Know …

# …About the Censorship of Mail in Bermuda during World War II?

Whereas the censorship of Bermuda's terminal mail began at the outset of the war, transit mail on neutral ships was not censored until later in 1939 and mail carried by the Pan American Airways flying boats until 18 January 1940 when 112 bags of mail were removed from PAA *American Clipper*. That mail included securities, packages of diamonds and large money transfers from Germany – one alone of $300,000. With its first-class harbour and recently-opened flying boat base at Darrell's Island, Bermuda proved the ideal location for the censorship of trans-Atlantic mail.

Both the United States and Germany were very unhappy with Great Britain's interference with their mail. On 27 January 1940, Berlin Radio blasted Bermuda, claiming that it was rightly called the 'Island of Devils' and that this 'home of pirates, buccaneers and thieves now lives up to its vile reputation by pirating mail'. Meanwhile the U.S. Government decided to stop PAA trans-Atlantic flights from landing in Bermuda altogether.

By August 1940 the U.S. Government reversed course and decided 'there would be compensating advantages from mail censorship at Bermuda'. Additional censors would soon arrive and the Imperial Censorship Detachment was established at the Inverurie Hotel, close to the Darrell's Island airport. The censorship of transit mail, examination of travellers' possessions and control of contraband was now fully operational and neutral shipping subject to examination.

Facilities at the Inverurie Hotel were soon outgrown and on 22 September 1940, coincidentally with the arrival of 200 more examiners from Great Britain, the Imperial Censorship Detachment moved operations to the more spacious Princess Hotel in Hamilton, which was ideally located to receive and dispatch transit mail that arrived by sea or air.

In all, 1,500 censors and 'censorettes' were in Bermuda during the four years of operation. Only twenty-four would stay behind when the Imperial Censorship Detachment left Bermuda in 1944.

*Censors at work at the Princess Hotel during World War II*

Most were women who stayed to marry, a few were over sixty and decided to retire in Bermuda, five were employed by the Bermuda Government, two by the United States Navy and two remained to assist with Prize Court proceedings.

Bermuda Censorship could examine 200,000 letters per day and could submit 15,000 to clinical testing by special examiners looking for microdots and secret ink messages. Some of the information gained from letters led to the successful prosecution of the Ludwig spy ring and the conviction of the notorious pro-German propagandist George Viereck, especially when FBI activities were still restricted by American neutrality. Through its Contraband Control Bermuda also caused considerable damage to the German economy and war effort. And all of this took place at the Princess Hotel!

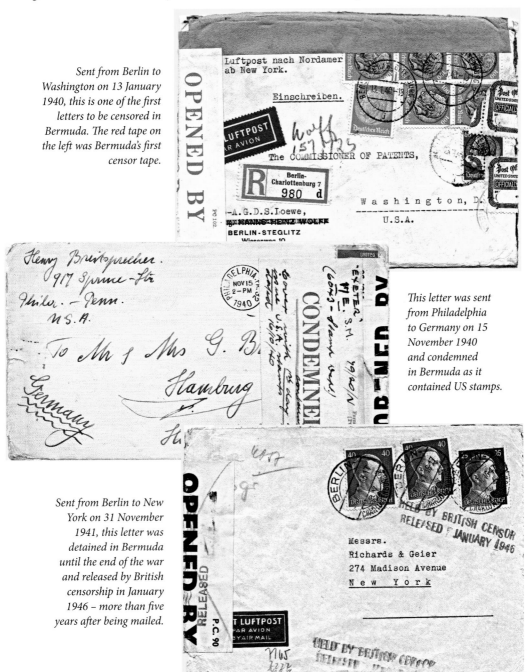

*Sent from Berlin to Washington on 13 January 1940, this is one of the first letters to be censored in Bermuda. The red tape on the left was Bermuda's first censor tape.*

*This letter was sent from Philadelphia to Germany on 15 November 1940 and condemned in Bermuda as it contained US stamps.*

*Sent from Berlin to New York on 31 November 1941, this letter was detained in Bermuda until the end of the war and released by British censorship in January 1946 – more than five years after being mailed.*

Do You Know …

# … That 635 Impressionist Paintings and Sketches were seized in Bermuda in October 1940?

The collection of impressionist works of art formed by well-known French art dealer and collector Ambroise Vollard was seized by the Germans after the occupation of Paris in 1940. Although they were not interested in modern art, German authorities recognized the commercial value of what they described as 'commercial art' and consigned the collection to Martin Fabiani, a Paris art dealer and protégé of Ambroise Vollard who had died in July 1939. The object was to raise much-needed dollar currency by selling the paintings in New York.

British Intelligence was tipped off about this scheme and suspected that Fabiani was acting as a German agent. When the collection was shipped from Lisbon to New York aboard the American Export Line's *Excalibur*, a British warship stationed in Bermuda was instructed by the Admiralty to intercept the *Excalibur* and to bring her into the Great Sound.

Much to the annoyance of the captain of the *Excalibur*, his ship was seized and anchored in the Great Sound on October 3rd, 1940. The well-known author, H. Montgomery Hyde, then Security Officer with Contraband Control and British Censorship in Bermuda, received instructions from London to remove the *Excalibur's* cargo as contraband.

*H. Montgomery Hyde in 1940. He was seconded to Bermuda by MI-6, Britain's secret service.*

When boarding the *Excalibur* together with Bermuda's Chief Customs Officer Rowe Spurling and his assistant Ralph Gauntlett, Mr. Hyde was confronted by a very uncooperative captain who announced that the ship's strong-room had been locked and welded shut with strips of steel. This did not discourage Mr. Hyde, however, as he immediately sent a signal to Dockyard, requesting a shipwright-welder be dispatched to the *Excalibur* as quickly as possible.

Fifteen minutes later Edward Pearce appeared with his oxy-acetylene gear and electric welding equipment and burned off the steel strips. With the strong-room finally open, the wooden crates containing the paintings were lowered over the side onto the Customs boat and taken to Hamilton for safe storage.

After consultation with the Attorney-General, Trounsell Gilbert, it was determined that the staggering number of pictures – including 429 paintings and drawings by Renoir, 68 paintings by Cezanne, 57 by Rouault, 13 by Gaugin, 7 by Degas and many more by Manet, Monet and Picasso – would be subject to Prize Court proceedings. Because of Bermuda's humid climate, it was considered unwise to keep the paintings on the island and they were sent to Ottawa's Canadian National Gallery for the duration of the war. On May 4th, 1949, they were released to the original consignee, Martin Fabiani, the suspected German agent.

*The American Export Line's 'Excalibur' which had earlier brought the Duke and Duchess of Windsor to Bermuda.*

British Security Co-ordination

1940-1945

Certificate of Service

Lt. Col. Harford Montgomery Hyde

a member of British Security Co-ordination, has

performed valuable service of a confidential nature.

Wm Stephenson

Director

*Sir William Stephenson, CC, MC, DFC was Director of British Security Co-ordination during World War II. He was code-named 'Intrepid'. After the war he issued this Certificate of Service to Lt. Col. Harford Montgomery Hyde for 'valuable services of a confidential nature'. Sir William was a long term resident of Bermuda until his death in 1989.*

Do You Know ...

# ...That the only German submarine ever captured at sea was kept hidden in Bermuda?

U-505, a long-range German IX-C type submarine operated from Lorient, France, and was based in the South Atlantic and credited with sinking 47,000 tons of allied shipping. In early June 1944, with the help of radio transmission intercepts, U-505 was tracked near the Cape Verde Islands. A US Navy Task Group consisting of the escort carrier *USS Guadalcanal* and five destroyers operated in the area and was sent to intercept.

On June 4, 1944, the destroyer *USS Chatelain* reported a sonar contact 800 yards away and immediately covered the area with depth charges. Aboard the U-505, Oberleutnant Harald Lange, the submarine's commander, attempted to maneuver to safety, however, power was lost and the rudder was jammed to starboard. Captain Lange had no option but to surface and abandon ship. Ordering the U-Boat to be scuttled, Captain Lange and his crew began to abandon the submarine which continued to circle at about seven knots, slowly filling with water.

While the *USS Chatelain* and *USS Jenks* were picking up survivors, the *USS Pillsbury* sent a nine-man boarding party to the submarine. Despite the probability of the U-505 sinking or blowing up at any moment, the boarding party quickly climbed down the hatch and found that the submarine had been deserted. After disconnecting scuttle charges and closing valves, the boarding party managed to retrieve important codebooks and the Enigma machine itself. Only one German sailor was killed during the capture of U-505. The remaining 58 crew members were all rescued from the sea.

It was the first time since the War of 1812 that U.S. forces captured an enemy ship on the high seas. It was also the first time that a German submarine was ever captured at sea.

Because Allied leadership was worried that if the Germans found out that one of their

*A salvage party tries to keep crippled U-505 afloat after its capture.*

*The U-505 at the Naval Operating Base in Southampton with a US Navy flying boat landing in the Great Sound.*

submarines had been captured, they would know that the Allies had broken the Enigma codes. It was therefore decided to tow U-505 to Bermuda. The Task Force turned west and, towed by the fleet tug *USS Abnaki,* the prize arrived in Bermuda on June 19, 1944. Shrouded in secrecy, U-505 remained in Bermuda until the end of the war. To further protect the secret, the prisoners from U-505 were kept in Bermuda for several weeks and later sent to a prison camp in Louisiana, while the Germans were told that they had all been killed in battle.

After the war, efforts were made to save U-505 as a museum and since 1954 the submarine has been on exhibit at the Chicago Museum of Science & Industry. She is the only surviving Type IX-C long-range U-Boat in the world.

*U-505 hidden in Bermuda next to the fleet tug USS Abnaki.*
*Photos courtesy of the Chicago Museum of Science & Industry.*

Do You Know ...

# ... That Bermuda's first six buses were green and only cost $1,000?

With the demise of the Bermuda Railway, the Bermuda Government in 1946 purchased six second-hand 21-seater General Motors Corporation Model 733 buses from New Jersey Public Service Coordinated for the grand total of $1,000.

These American-made buses were left-hand drive, which meant that the public had to get on and off the buses on the road, rather than the sidewalk! Eventually two of the six buses had the passenger door relocated to the other side. The buses were also repainted green in Bermuda.

*This Royal Gazette photo, taken on Front Street in Hamilton, shows passengers getting on the bus on the farside of the vehicle.*

The first bus service – from Hamilton to Tucker's Town – got under way on Tuesday, April 23rd, 1946. There was little ceremony and there were no passengers on the 7.00am bus. When it returned to Hamilton at 8:30am, it carried 18 fare-paying passengers.

*A Morris bus at the bottom of Spurling Hill, before the rails of the Bermuda Railway were removed.*
*Photo: Bermudian Publishing Ltd.*

When the Bermuda Railway finally shut down, it was felt that Bermuda needed a minimum of 28 buses to provide island-wide service and 20 Morris Commercial Model CVF13/5 buses were imported from England at a cost of £2,025 each.

On arrival in Bermuda four of the 24 seats were removed as it was felt that the buses were too cramped. At first the buses were painted beige with a green waist band, but later they were painted in two distinct tones of green.

By 1950 well over 5,000 passengers were carried on Bermuda's buses on a daily basis and larger buses were urgently needed. The choice was for the Seddon all-aluminium body 31-passenger Model Mk 4. They were again painted green. From 1950 until 1978 all of Bermuda's buses were made by Seddon. Starting in 1965 they were painted pink.

For more detailed information on Bermuda's buses see 'The Buses of Bermuda' by Colin A. Pomeroy and Michael J. Herbert. It is available at local bookstores.

*A Seddon Mk 10 bus of the early 1960's in Market Square in St. George's.*

*Modern Bermuda buses.*

Do You Know ...

# ... About the making of a Stamp Issue –
# 50 years ago?

2012 is not only the 200th Anniversary of Bermuda's Postal Service, but also the 50th Anniversary of the 'Buildings Definitives', a set of Bermuda postage stamps which was acclaimed internationally as 'a set which is unlike any that has gone before'.

During 1961 Bermuda's Colonial Treasurer, the Hon. W.W. Davidson, announced that a complete new issue of Bermuda stamps was to be introduced in 1962 to replace Bermuda's first Elizabethan definitive stamps issued in 1953. That set, the result of a public design competition, was criticized as being a 'hotchpotch of everybody's notions on how a stamp should look'.

Consequently local artist William H. Harrington decided to submit 21 uniform designs showing Bermuda buildings and proposed that they be printed in the photogravure printing process, a printing method most suitable to reproduce the delicate colours that Bermuda is so well known for. The disadvantage of photogravure in not being able to reproduce type and lines with sharp clean edges was considered of less importance.

Mr. Harrington's sketches, 12.5" x 19" inches in size, were basically pencil drawings with just a hint of colour. Once 17 designs were selected, the basic art and border were painted in colour

*The 17 'Buildings Definitives' stamps issued on October 26th, 1962.*

on heavy card, 6" x 4.5" in size. An overlay was then added for the type and crown, as well as the photograph of Queen Elizabeth II.

Shown here, as an example, are the various components of the £1 stamp:

*William Harrington's sketch of the House of Assembly – the proposed £1 stamp. The sketch shows where Mr. Harrington made changes, for example, he originally placed '£1' in front of 'Bermuda'. The biggest change was to use the Queen's Head for the final stamps, rather than the Royal Cypher as originally planned. The St. Edward's Crown was also changed to better suit the design of the stamps.*

*The basic artwork painted in colour.*

*The 'line overlay' with type and crown, combined with the 'halftone overlay' of the Queen's Head, a portrait by Dorothy Wilding.*

*A combination of the artwork with the various overlays. Unfortunately Mr. Harrington was not able to see his design this way as the technology was not available in 1962.*

When the Buildings Issue was released on October 26th, 1962, the stamps caused great excitement in the philatelic press worldwide. Comments like these were not unusual: 'these stamps set a new and attractive style in colonial stamp design'; 'all collectors of British Commonwealth stamps are getting a thrill out of this issue'; 'the new set is a handsome replacement for the previous one and will add colour and interest to many a collector's album'; 'there's a tip of the hat due Bermuda for the colourful new definitive issue'.

## Do You Know …

# … The more flawed they are, the more valuable they become!

It's a funny thing about stamps, when something goes wrong during the production process, collectors get eager to open their wallets – the opposite of what normally happens when something isn't perfect.

Flaws fall into these main categories: Omitted Colours and Partially Omitted Colours; Colour Shifts; Doctor Blade Flaws; Perforation Errors and Watermark Errors.

*'3d' and 'BERMUDA' was omitted on some 'Olympic' stamps sold at the General Post Office in 1968.*

*A few 15¢ stamps of the 1973 'Tree Issue' sold at the Reefs Hotel for mailing postcards were missing the brown ink of the 'Queen's Head' and '15¢' value.*

The total omission of one colour in multi-colour printing can occur for two reasons – a sheet is either not put through the printing press during the printing of one colour; or two sheets went through the printing press together, with the result that the bottom sheet missed the colour being printed at that time.

*The brown ink of Government House was omitted on one row of the 3d stamps issued in 1962.*

*When $3 stamps of the Wildlife series were overprinted 90¢, one stamp missed the overprint.*

Partially omitted colours on a sheet of stamps can either occur at start-up when the impression cylinder is first engaged, transferring the ink to the paper, or when the press is stopped and the impression cylinder is disengaged to deal with a problem such as a paper jam.

*During the printing of the orange colour of the 1/- 'Buildings Issue' in 1962, one sheet was not aligned properly and resulted in this striking 12mm colour shift.*

Colour shifts occur when a press sheet is not properly aligned in the feeder of the printing press and can result is dramatic colour shifts.

*Two examples of doctor blade flaws on the 2/- 'Buildings Issue' of 1962 and the $1.20 'Flower' stamps of 1970. The thickness of the foreign matter in the ink determines the width of the ink flare. These flaws are always on a slight angle as the doctor blade oscillates during printing to prevent these errors as much as possible.*

In photogravure printing doctor blades exert firm pressure against the cylinder surface during the rotation of the cylinder, removing all excess ink. If foreign matter gets stuck under the blade, allowing ink to pass on either side of the flaw, it can result in rather striking flaws.

*Missing perforations on the 2d and a freak error on the 6d stamps of the 'Buildings Issue' of 1962.*

*The perforations were completely missing from one sheet of the 1970 'Flower' issue.*

*The top two rows of one sheet of the 40¢ 'Education' issue of 1997 sold at the Flatts Post Office missed the perforation.*

Perforation errors can be equally striking and occur when sheets are either not perforated at all, or when part of a sheet fails to enter the comb perforator. Occasionally freak perforation errors occur when a sheet is partly folded over.

As stamps are printed on watermarked security paper, errors occur if sheets of paper are fed through the printing press up-side-down. Although not visible to the naked eye, they are very collectible. In fact, it is well worth keeping a lookout for flaws and errors on Bermuda stamps as some of them can be quite valuable.

Do You Know …

# … About Bermuda's only Papal Visit?

On Saturday, August 24th, 1968, Pope Paul VI paid a short visit to Bermuda following his trip to Bogota, Colombia, to attend the 39th Eucharistic Congress. It was the only Papal Visit to our island.

About 5,000 people gathered at the airport to greet the Pontiff when he stepped out of the aircraft at 11:30 p.m. Welcomed by Bermuda's Catholic Bishop, the Most Rev. Bernard J. Murphy and H.E. the Governor, Lord Martonmere, the welcoming party walked to a flower-decked dais on the tarmac where a number of dignitaries were presented to the Pope.

In his welcoming speech Lord Martonmere said "There are days in the life of every country when history is made – this is such a day. People of many faiths have come here tonight to pay tribute to a Pope who is not only a great religious leader but also a great apostle of world peace and human understanding". Pope Paul replied: "How strange it would have seemed until recently that the Successor of St. Peter would find sufficient a few hours to cross broad continents and mighty seas, and visit distant lands whose very existence was unknown to the first Pope!"

Following an exchange of various gifts, the 70-year old Pope Paul, surrounded by police and his own security men, then walked briskly into the crowded airport building and through to the VIP lounge for a short rest and talk with Bishop Murphy. "We spoke about Bermuda and His Holiness expressed great interest in the welfare of the Church here" said Bishop Murphy.

Pope Paul VI reigned as Pope of the Catholic Church from 1963 to 1978. Succeeding Pope John XXIII, he fostered improved ecumenical relations with Orthodox, Anglicans and Protestants, which resulted in many historic meetings and agreements. He took the name Paul to indicate a renewed worldwide mission to spread the message of Christ. He re-opened the Second Vatican Council and gave it priority and direction. After the Council concluded its work, Paul VI took charge of the interpretation and implementation of its mandates, often walking a thin line between the conflicting expectations of various groups within the Roman Catholic Church.

The magnitude and depth of the reforms affecting all areas of Church life during his pontificate exceeded similar reform policies of his predecessors. His positions on birth control and other issues were controversial in Western Europe and North America, but were applauded by people in Eastern and Southern Europe and Latin America. His pontificate took place during sometimes revolutionary changes in the world, student revolts, the Vietnam War and other upheavals.

*A souvenir cover issued by the Vatican, showing the special Bermuda cancellation and flight route from Bogota to Bermuda and then on to Rome.*

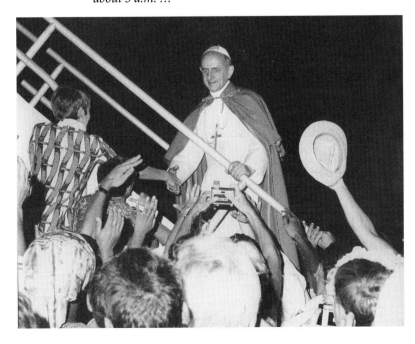

*Pope Paul, surrounded by his private security and Bermuda policemen, walks to the airport building. To his right is Bermuda's Bishop Bernard J. Murphy and H.E. the Governor, Lord Martonmere.*

*Back to the plane at about 3 a.m. …*

Photos by Horst Augustinovic

*… and a final farewell to a cheering crowd before boarding the Avianca jet.*

Do You Know …

# … How many of Bermuda's Roads are named in honour of Cricket?

Cricket, a centuries-old game that originated in England, was first brought to Bermuda in the 1840s by soldiers of the British Army. A match played in St. George's between the Army Garrison team and members of the Royal Navy at Dockyard started to make cricket the popular sport it is today. In 1855 the Bermuda Cricket Club was founded in St. George's and the first game was played against the Army Garrison team.

As Bermudians of all backgrounds fell in love with the game – but still lacked proper cricket gear – substitutes were made. Oleander trees were particularly good to carve a bat and a stone wrapped in cloth made a suitable ball. And the game was on. On one such occasion a number of boys playing in Somerset were approached by a group of Naval officers who asked if they could join in the game. The batter was no other than HRH Prince George, later to become King George V!

And it wasn't just cricket gear which was lacking early on, proper 'cricket pitches' were also not available to most players. According to William Zuill in 'Bermuda Journey', Johnny Fox of St. David's came up with a novel method to keep his field in order. He built a big wire cage, something like a fishpot, with a door large enough to admit a goat. Once inside, the goat began to crop grass and continued the good work until the cage was moved to another spot. This way the ground was always ready for play with a minimum of effort.

It wasn't until the formation of the all-black Bermuda Militia Artillery in 1890 that Bermudians were able to play regularly with proper cricket gear against British Army and Royal Navy teams. Being selected for any of these Inter-Service matches soon became a distinct honour for Bermudian cricketers.

Forty years after the abolition of slavery in Bermuda on August 1st, 1834 – Emancipation Day – Captain J. Moresby of the Royal Navy began an unofficial two-day sporting tradition with cricket matches played between two fraternal lodges from the opposite ends of the island.

These matches between the two lodges of the Grand United Order of Oddfellows were so popular, that following the 1901 game at which one team won by only one run, it was agreed that a Cup should be played for annually. In 1902 three two-innings games were to be played in June, July and August, with the Cup going to the winner of the best of the three games. Unfortunately the 1902 game had to be abandoned in a brawl.

It was then decided that as of 1903 there would only be

one game and the winner was to hold the Cup until it was won by the other side. This 'winner–take-all' concept worked well when both teams were relatively balanced, however, when one side had a string of victories – like Somerset in the 1930s and 1940s – and the Cup was played at the same club for a number of years, the opposite side began to feel the resulting loss of revenue. It was therefore decided that the game could not be played for more than two years at the same club. Even this proved unsatisfactory and the decision was finally made to alternate on an annual basis, regardless of which side held the Cup.

While initially only the first day of Cup Match – now Emancipation Day – was a public holiday, absenteeism from work on the second day became such a serious problem, that in 1947 the two-day public holiday was introduced. And ever since Bermuda is the only country in the world where everything comes to a grinding halt for two days every summer, and almost everyone's attention turns to the game of cricket.

So how many of our roads are named in honour of cricket? By some accounts there are four – Fielders Lane in Smith's Parish, near the Flatts Victoria Cricket Club, as well as three in Sandys Parish – Bat'n'Ball Lane, Cricket Lane, and Grandstand Lane, all near the Somerset Cricket Club. If you know of any others, I'd like to know.

*In 1976 the Bermuda Post Office issued four stamps to commemorate the*
*75th Anniversary of Cup Match in Bermuda.*

Do You Know …

# … That Alfred Birdsey was also a lithographer?

Lithography was accidentally invented in 1798 by Alois Senefelder in Solnhofen, Bavaria, Germany, while he was experimenting with copperplate engraving on the cheaper Bavarian limestone, rather than expensive copper. The principle on which lithography is based is the fact that water and greasy substances repel each other and for the next 100+ years the stones from the Solnhofen quarry were the preferred stones for the lithographic printing process.

*Bermuda's well-known artist Alfred Birdsey*

The technical details of printing from stones were quite complicated. At the beginning there were neither lithographic presses, nor inks or chemicals available for purchase. The art was quite primitive and difficult to learn, and successful lithographers did not easily divulge their trade secrets.

The preparation of the stone, creating the image, inking and dampening, preparing the paper, and finally making the impression were all manually performed. Still, a good lithographer was first and foremost a graphic artist, and in many cases a creative artist. Alfred Birdsey was certainly in this category.

Having moved to Bermuda in 1919 when he was only 7 years old, Alfred Birdsey became an entirely self-taught artist. Mentored, however, by two American artists – Donald Kirkpatrick and Joe Jones. In the 1950s Alfred developed his interest in oriental art as seen in the characteristic watercolours for which he is best known.

In the late 1950s he became interested in lithography and, lacking a proper lithographic stone, experimented unsuccessfully with marble. According to his daughter Jo Birdsey-Linberg, he was offered two stones by a printer in New York and he and his family travelled there on the *Queen of Bermuda* to collect the precious stones. Next he had to master the chemistry involved. Polishing the stone with pumice powder, neutralizing it with nitric acid and finally preserving the surface with gum Arabic.

Of course Alfred also lacked a printing press and this is where his future son-in-law – Sjur Linberg – came into the picture. Being an architect, Alfred asked him to build a very basic press to make single-colour impressions. Multi-colour printing would have required a more sophisticated machine allowing for proper registration of colours. That is the reason why Alfred Birdsey's lithographs are printed in one colour only, with perhaps some colour wash added later.

Yes, Alfred Birdsey loved to experiment with his watercolour and oil paintings for which he is know worldwide. His interest in lithography, however, makes him unique as Bermuda's only true lithographer.

*An early lithographic printing press showing the stone and pressure cylinder for transferring the printing ink to the paper*

*Birdsey by Birdsey*
*– a rare self-portrait by the artist*

*A Birdsey nude – a rather unusual*
*subject for Alfred Birdsey*

*Alfred Birdsey's 'blue period', when he*
*used blue printing ink rather than the*
*usual black ink*

*A more traditional Birdsey scene,*
*drawn in reverse on his stone and*
*then printed in ink, rather than*
*painted in watercolour or oil*

Do You Know …

# … About the origin of Rugby Week, College Weeks, Spring Break and Bermuda's Green Ticket?

Apparently the tradition of American students going somewhere tropical during spring break began in 1935 when The Bermuda Athletic Association invited Harvard, Yale and Princeton's rugby teams to come to Bermuda for a friendly scrum, offering the students a $50 travel stipend. The spring break tradition of sun and sport was born. By the 1950's Rugby Week became known as College Week, and later Spring Break.

In 1948 Life Magazine covered the Bermuda Rugby Week in a cover story proclaiming, "It is one continuous party for 500 US collegians." Soon Bermuda became an annual springtime playground for elite Ivy Leaguers – and those who hoped to marry them.  But by the late 1950s rising college

*As this Bermuda Sun cartoon by John Miles shows, the Bermuda Police was rather uneasy about the annual arrival of College Kids.*

enrollment and affluence allowed the masses to crash the party and the seven days of revelry became known simply as College Week.

According to Life Magazine, the co-eds "got terribly tangled up riding bicycles in the left-hand Bermuda traffic. They got terrible sunburns, and most of them saw little of Bermuda. But for the tourist-conscious Bermudians, Rugby Week was sure to pay off. They can expect to meet at least one fourth of the collegians again – as honeymooners." Many of them did.

> **MAY WE RESPECTFULLY SUGGEST THAT YOUR ATTIRE MAY PROVE TO BE EMBARRASSING AS THERE ARE CERTAIN REGULATIONS PERTAINING TO PROPRIETY OF DRESS THAT ARE BEING ENFORCED IN ORDER TO MAINTAIN BERMUDA'S POSITION AS A MOST ATTRACTIVE AND PLEASANT HOLIDAY RESORT.**

*Bermuda's Green Ticket*

During the 1950's and 1960's Bermudians and visitors alike were expected to adhere to a strict dress code and students here during college week often came into conflict with that idea. Police Officers were directed to tactfully issue a notice called a 'Green Ticket' to anyone they considered to be improperly dressed in public. For example if they felt that the length of a woman's skirt was too short, or if her shorts were, well - too short!

In 1962 a U.S. newspaper reported that a Hamilton police constable, while measuring a young lady's shorts, turned ruddy red right up to his helmet when she threw her arms around him and implored, "Henry, let's get married right away." And so the Green Tickets were largely ignored and instead became treasured souvenirs to hang on a sorority house wall.

But not just short shorts were taboo. So were hair curlers. This calypso was commissioned by the Trade Development Board and supposed to rid Bermuda streets of tourist hair curlers:

> In Bermuda, it's taboo
> Look out: don't let the cops
>     catch you.
> Keep your curlers out of
>     sight
> Don't let 'em show in
>     broad daylight.
> Pretty girls are super fine
> But no one loves a
>     porcupine …

*Constable Robert Wooley measures the length of actress Eunice Gayson's shorts in this publicity photo taken by the Bermuda News Bureau*